Brian Moore

THE IRISH WRITERS SERIES
James F. Carens, General Editor

TITLE	*AUTHOR*
SEAN O'CASEY	Bernard Benstock
J. C. MANGAN	James Kilroy
W. R. RODGERS	Darcy O'Brien
STANDISH O'GRADY	Phillip L. Marcus
PAUL VINCENT CARROLL	Paul A. Doyle
SEUMAS O'KELLY	George Brandon Saul
SHERIDAN LEFANU	Michael Begnal
BRIAN FRIEL	D. E. S. Maxwell
DANIEL CORKERY	George Brandon Saul
EIMAR O'DUFFY	Robert Hogan
MERVYN WALL	Robert Hogan
FRANK O'CONNOR	James Matthews
JOHN BUTLER YEATS	Douglas Archibald
MARIA EDGEWORTH	James Newcomer
MARY LAVIN	Zack Bowen
SOMERVILLE AND ROSS	John Cronin
SUSAN L. MITCHELL	Richard M. Kain
J. M. SYNGE	Robin Skelton
KATHARINE TYNAN	Marilyn Gaddis Rose
LIAM O'FLAHERTY	James O'Brien
IRIS MURDOCH	Donna Gerstenberger
BENEDICT KIELY	Daniel J. Casey
DOUGLAS HYDE	Gareth Dunleavy
EDNA O'BRIEN	Grace Eckley
BRIAN MOORE	Jeanne Flood
ELIZABETH BOWEN	Edwin J. Kenney
JOHN MONTAGUE	Frank Kersnowski
CHARLES ROBERT MATURIN	Robert E. Lougy

GEORGE FITZMAURICE	Arthur E. McGuinness
FRANCIS STUART	J. H. Natterstad
PATRICK KAVANAGH	Darcy O'Brien
WILLIAM ALLINGHAM	Alan Warner
SIR SAMUEL FERGUSON	Malcolm Brown
LADY GREGORY	Hazard Adams
GEORGE RUSSELL (AE)	Richard M. Kain and
	James O'Brien
THOMAS DAVIS	Eileen Sullivan
PEADAR O'DONNELL	Grattan Freyer
OLIVER ST. JOHN GOGARTY	J. B. Lyons
SEUMAS HEANEY	Robert Buttel

BRIAN MOORE

Jeanne Flood

Lewisburg
BUCKNELL UNIVERSITY PRESS
London: Associated University Presses

© 1974 by Associated University Presses, Inc.

Associated University Presses, Inc.
Cranbury, New Jersey 08512

Associated University Presses
108 New Bond Street
London W1Y OQX, England

Library of Congress Cataloging in Publication Data

Flood, Jeanne.
  Brian Moore.

  (The Irish writers series)
  Bibliography: p.
  1. Moore, Brian—Criticism and interpretation.
PR6063.06Z63   813'.5'4   76–168808
ISBN 0–8387–7823–2
ISBN 0–8387–7972–7 (pbk.)

Contents

Chronology

1957	Publication of *The Feast of Lupercal*
1959	Moves to the United States; receives Guggenheim Fellowship
1960	Publication of *The Luck of Ginger Coffey*
1962	Publication of *An Answer From Limbo*
1966	Publication of *The Emperor of Ice Cream;* now married to Jean Denny
1968	Publication of *I Am Mary Dunne*
1970	Publication of *Fergus*
1971	Publication of *The Revolution Script*
1972	Publication of *Catholics*

1

The Novelist in Disguise

At the end of Brian Moore's most recent novel, *Catholics* (New York, 1973), an abbot kneels in front of the tabernacle in the abbey church to lead his monks in prayer. He believes the tabernacle to be empty; he knows that the effect of his prayer will be his own experience of horror at the emptiness of the universe. In Moore's first book published in 1955, a neurotic spinster appalled by her growing conviction that the tabernacle is empty, blasphemously assaults it in an effort to discover if God is inside. The question of the vacancy of the tabernacle or its overwhelming fullness lies at the center of Moore's work, for to that question are tied two others with which he has struggled in his novels, out of which he has created his novels. With the fullness of the tabernacle, Moore associates an objective world which is created and ordered by a father whose absolute power is synonymous with a terrible sadistic energy. With its emptiness he associates a void in which a person floats, trapped forever in his own solipsistic dream. On the great presence or the great absence depend the reality of the world outside the mind and the legitimacy of the novelist's commitment to his own imagination.

The creating of fictions is the central subject of the seven novels Moore published between 1955 and 1970. In each of them, he presents a single character whose every vital energy is given to a private life in fantasy. That character, no matter the facts of biography or of sexual designation, is very strongly identified with Moore the novelist, although it is not until his fourth book that the fantasizer emerges as a novelist. In each of the first four books, the dream life of the central character is a guilty one, for he has treacherously withdrawn from the morally valid world of the father; in each book he is rightly punished for that betrayal. Yet the world which the fantasizer has denied is one in which he has been brutally humiliated by the very power which has created it—and created him. As Moore develops as a writer, the rebellion of the fantasizer against the father as God becomes personalized, explicitly attached to Moore himself and to his complex relation to his own father. In his first two books, however, the fantasizer's struggle against reality and defeat by it are presented through a study of the lives of two aging and powerless celibates in the Belfast Catholic community. Both characters are carefully dissociated from Moore personally. "I wanted my major character to be someone who wasn't me—who could never be mistaken for me," he said in an interview about the creation of Judith Hearne. "And yet," he adds, "I was lonely for much of my life, and so I put something of myself into her." (Hallvard Dahlie, "An Interview With Brian Moore," *Tamarack Review,* Winter, 1968, p. 15.) The rebellious artist is disguised in these first two books as a spinster alcoholic and an impotent schoolmaster; the overwhelming father is hidden in the powerful social institutions of Catholic Belfast—family, church, school. The concealment gives the apparently dispassionate realistic studies of two wasted lives in a restricted provincial town an extraordinary intensity.

Judith Hearne (London, 1955) begins and ends with Miss Hearne placing in the lodgings where she has currently come to rest her personal symbols for family and religion: a picture of her dead aunt and a picture of the Sacred Heart. Between the two occasions lies the crisis in which she has recognized the destructiveness of both forces in her life. At the end, as in the beginning however, she clings to them as the organizing centers of her world; they protect her from chaos. She reflects first in her shabby rented room in the boarding house of Mrs. Henry Rice and then in her sanitarium bed, after the installation of the pictures: "When they're with me, watching over me, a new place becomes home." (pages 18 and 223.)

There is only one figure in the desolate history of Judith Hearne's first thirty-six years—the aunt, who had taken in the orphaned Judith Hearne as a child, and then ruthlessly used the grown woman for companion and nurse during her own decline into incontinent senility. On the aunt's death, Miss Hearne is in an all but hopeless situation. She is almost friendless, desperately poor, and pathetically unable to deal with the practical difficulties of managing her own life. Worst of all, she is mired in a decayed childhood, given to little anthropomorphic games and bedtime rituals in which she says her prayers and bids fond goodnight to the talismanic pictures. She suffers agonies over the simplest social exchanges, but matches her awkward self-consciousness with the child's utter lack of real self-awareness. She avoids recognition of her own alcoholism and her sexual frustration. Her usual refuge from the bitter deprivation of her life is in a daydream of a gracious future with a rich and loving, if unidentified person, of whom she thinks as Mr. Right.

The precipitating factor in the crisis in her life which the book explores is her romance with James Madden, who is the brother of her landlady and who has recently returned, apparently wealthy, from living in America. After meeting him at her first breakfast in the Rice boarding house, simply because he has spoken kindly to her, she creates a vision of her married life with him which combines her childishness and her masochism; she sees herself perched prettily on his knee, and then staggering from a punishing slap. Partly out of loneliness, partly out of half-hearted financial scheming, Madden begins to pay attention to her, and her fantasies assume a dominating certainty.

The word "passion" in the title of the American edition of the book indicates the dimension of sex and the dimension of suffering in the experience of Judith Hearne which constitutes the action of the novel. The first sense suggests Miss Hearne's pathetic infatuation with Madden, the second her total humiliation and breakdown. The first seven chapters of the book explore the romantic fantasies which signify to her passion in its sexual sense. The peak of her happiness is reached on the night that she mistakes Madden's proposition for a business partnership in a hamburger stand for a tentative proposal of marriage. That very same night, however, her experience of passion as suffering begins. The Rices, mother and son, reveal to her that Madden was the doorman of a New York hotel, not, as Miss Hearne had thought, its manager. Shocked by this disclosure, she goes to her room, turns the sacred pictures to the wall, and unlocks a secret cache of whiskey. The self-destructive drinking begins, it should be noticed, not because Madden has actually broken with her, but because in learning the truth about his class status, she has her first intimation of his reality as a person.

Having entered into this second form of passion, she spares herself no humiliation. She gets loudly drunk in the boarding house and engages in a series of degrading scenes. She confronts Madden, insists on marriage, and listens to him obliterate her last shreds of dignity and of hope. Beneath the deteriorating social surface of her life, the religious certainties on which it has been built begin to crack. She experiences doubt for the first time, and though terrified and guilty about her doubt, she cannot shake it off. She sees herself in a new perspective of waste and loss. If God does not exist, then Miss Hearne, faithful niece, has thrown away her life. "Nobody at all up above me, watching over me. Then nothing is sinful. There is no sin. And I have been cheated. . . ." (p. 124) In the moment that she doubts, she thinks of sex, remembering a book from Paris she had once seen, a boy in bathing trunks, a doctor who had once examined her; she fantasizes spectacular rapes.

Moore shows her provoke and endure a series of social and spiritual evictions as her desperation grows. She is forced out of one place after another: first, the Rice boarding house, then a sanitarium where she has gone to visit the woman who introduced her to the pleasures of alcohol, then the house of the O'Neills, the last of the old family friends. In an effort to establish the fact of God's existence and thus to locate herself somewhere in the universe, if not in the community, she tries to cause God to reveal himself by forcing him to punish her. This objective motivates the disastrous final spree, which impoverishes her both literally and figuratively. When God remains obstinately silent, she goes to Father Quigley, the pastor of her parish, and begs him to assure her of God's existence. Once more, she is ejected; he sends her away to sober up, speeding her with a stern reprimand. In desperation she goes into the church and screams "I hate You," (p. 209) begging for the obliteration which will justify her life. Goaded to the ultimate blasphemy, she tries to open the tabernacle door: "Open. Let me in!" she cries, scrabbling at the door till her fingers bleed. Then she gets what she has asked for:

> He came out, terrible, breathing fire, His face hollow-cheeked, His eyes devouring her. His Mother ran up the altar steps, her painted face still sadly smiling, lifted her as she lay broken on the steps. Saint Joseph knelt gravely on her right.
>
> And He, His fingers uplifted in blessing, bent over her, His bleeding heart red against His white tunic. Lifted her in His arms and His face was close to her. (p. 211)

Her hallucination has converted Father Quigley into the Sacred Heart and two housewives into Mary and Joseph. The child in the creche is Judith Hearne, but she is also the corpse in the Pieta.

The tableau on the altar is the most vivid and concentrated statement of the dynamic of family and religion in Judith Hearne's life. When Father Quigley holds her in his arms, she experiences the second powerful embrace of her life. The first occurred years before when the crazed aunt, having insured Miss Hearne's bondage, crushed her against the folds of her soiled night dress in a grotesque parody of love. (p. 112) The Sacred Heart and the aunt —religion and family—form one overwhelming parental force which demands submission and obedience. Miss Hearne is victim *because* she is child.

A Sunday sermon given by Father Quigley shows the existence in terms of the whole Catholic community of the same powerful demands for renunciation and obedience. The redoubtable pastor of St. Finbar's vigorously exercises his parental power. The sermon is a lengthy reproach-threat against a congregation of adult Catholics, "You that's jiggling your feet and rubbing the backs of your heads along the fresh paint that was put on the walls." (p. 62) He begins by promising that the "hooliganism" of the parishioners will no longer be tolerated, and ends by announcing that henceforth they will be locked in the church of a Sunday for their own immortal welfare. Their "disrespect to the Holy Tabernacle and the Blessed Body of Our Lord" (p. 62) will cease, he says, and he launches into a long accusation. Essentially the parishioners are guilty of preferring the pleasures of time and the body to the certainties of eternity. They are accused of going to films, pubs, dog races, football matches; of buying clothes, using cosmetics, smoking cigarettes, and reading books and magazines. The point of the sermon is clear: people are guilty of their most innocent personal gratifications; they are exhorted to renounce in favor of eternity, to give to God, to deny themselves. The parishioners are dirty, noisy, and bad. They are guilty and irresponsible children who will be punished for their own good. This frogmarch back to the humiliations of childhood is justified and endured by the congregation in the name of God and of man's immortal soul. The lifelong submission and renunciation of Judith Hearne are justified on the same basis. Family and religion are complementary parts of a powerful mechanism which obliterates the drives and hungers of the individual person in the service of the larger units of life in the Catholic community. Desires for individual fulfillment, as the sermon shows, are by definition evil in this context. Thus, Judith Hearne must repent in tears her only effort to free herself of the life-destroying burden of her aunt.

The sole refuge of the person trapped inside these grinding mechanisms is in fantasy. Aging, ugly, and poor, Judith Hearne is able to see herself as desirable and marriageable. It is the shattering of this vision of herself which drives her into crisis. Her alcoholism is simply another aspect of her dreaming. She drinks to stimulate her fantasizing powers, by means of which she is able to transform her experience in such a way as to make it tolerable. The narrative is quite explicit on this point:

> Drink was not to help forget, but to help remember, to clarify and arrange untidy and unpleasant facts into a perfect pattern of reasonableness and beauty. Alcoholic, she did not drink to put aside the dangers and disappointments of the moment. She drank to be able to see these trials more philosophically, to examine them more fully, fortified by the stimulant of unreason. (p. 106–107)

The fantasizing of the spinster alcoholic is very like the imaginative activity of the creative artist; Miss Hearne in arranging the grim facts of her life into humanly pleasing patterns does what the artist does.

In his presentation of the fantasies of Miss Hearne, Moore strikes a note which sounds through his first four books: imagination is the refuge of losers who cannot accommodate themselves to the mechanisms of the life into which they were born. An equally persisting attitude toward the imagination is introduced through the figure of Bernie Rice—parasite, sexual exploiter, manipulator, cynic, merciless egotist. He is the polar opposite of Judith Hearne; he has the qualities which would have freed her. Where she is exploited by family, he exploits it. She believes in God and renounces self-assertion; he sees religious belief as futile in terms of human life and remorselessly asserts himself. Yet both of them are perpetual children. At almost thirty years of age, Bernie, who looks "like some monstrous baby swelled to man size," (p. 9) is tenderly nurtured by his devoted mother, whose services extend to washing his hair.

Both Bernie Rice and Judith Hearne substitute imaginative activity for an adult role in society; Miss Hearne spends her life in fantasy, Bernie devotes himself to the writing of what he says is a great poem. Judith Hearne, who is so completely victimized by family and religion, is guilty of her inability to achieve an adult place for herself within the family system. At the same time, Bernie Rice, seeing the dangers of family and religion and protecting himself against them, is guilty of his refusal to assume such a place. Through the pairing of these antithetical figures, Moore suggests that withdrawal from the community into the isolated imagination is a contemptible regression to childhood. At the same time, however, he shows that the community insists that its adult members remain forever in a sanctioned childhood. The O'Neill family offers a case in point. Their drawing room is for the reader as well as the heroine an oasis of brightness in the gray misery of Belfast. The O'Neills offer Judith Hearne whatever human comforts she enjoys before her breakdown, and after it they are in fact paying her bills. The elder O'Neills are thus consistently adult. Yet within this family we notice that parental control, though loving and appropriate since the children are children, is rigid. The father of the family is a professor at Queen's University; he does not, however, read books on the Index, and he remarks to Miss Hearne, who is willing to forgive Chopin his liaison with George Sand for his music, that "Being an artist does not absolve a man from his religious duties." (p. 149) Owen O'Neill is a Catholic, and he follows the rules. We must therefore see him in the context of Father Quigley's sermon. No matter his position professionally and in his home, O'Neill's adulthood extends only as far as the parish church. To any priest, he is a child. If he belonged to St. Finbar's parish, he too would be locked in church between the offertory and the last gospel of the Sunday mass.

The conclusion is clear: whether the person stays within the community or withdraws from it into a private world, he can never achieve adult independence.

If he remains within the community, he has a chance for happiness, and he is guiltless. If he isolates himself in his own imagination, he is guilty of a shameful regression to childhood. The only person in the book who has physically left the community is Madden; his actual removal from Ulster has resulted in a total loss of hope and in his physical and emotional maiming. He has no status in any society; he is the absolutely displaced person.

The sympathetic treatment of the O'Neill family, a family which Moore has identified in an interview as "a sort of facsimile of my own," indicates the great attraction for Moore of the order and stability of the lives they lead. Judith Hearne has grasped, while she is testing God, the human terrors of living without the organizing points of family and religion. At her breakdown she becomes literally as well as metaphorically a child; she is passive in her hospital bed, but under the benign protection of the very forces which have crushed her. The community breaks its members, but it also guards them. It both destroys and protects the individual person.

The book does not resolve this contradition, and the reader is in effect trapped within it. In spite of a clear indictment of family and religion as the parts of a ruthlessly repressive mechanism, the presentation lof the sheer human decency and happiness of the O'Neill family justifies the system, and the values on which it is based. The reader must accept at one and the same time the irreconcilable notions that Judith Hearne's problems would have been solved if only she had been pretty enough and lucky enough to have attracted a good

Catholic husband, and that she cannot marry because she is the victim of repressive cultural forces. At the end of the book, Judith Hearne asks that the pictures of the Sacred Heart and her aunt be placed in her sanitarium room. The reader, who has seen that she has been destroyed by what the pictures represent, must also view this decision as the only adult act possible for her, in which she accepts in full knowledge her subservient place in the community and in which she exchanges the shameful childhood of living in fantasy for the sanctioned one of docile obedience. The reader is left at the end of the book in a state of painful confusion, a confusion I would suggest, which is the counterpart of Moore's ambivalence toward the ordered world over which his father presided. In his second book, *The Feast of Lupercal* (Boston, 1957), Moore solves the technical problems raised by this ambivalence. He creates as his victimized central character a person who, unlike Judith Hearne, does have a reasonable chance for happiness and whose inability to actualize that chance is rooted solely in the conditions which have formed his experience. Secondly, in St. Michan's College he creates a model which perfectly expresses his idea of paternity.

Diarmuid Devine, the hero of the book, is a thirty-seven year old bachelor English master at the College he himself had attended as a boy. He is perfectly adjusted to the school, knowing its routine so well that he can calculate the class periods to the minute without consulting his watch. His teaching is notable for the successful priming of boys for exams; his classroom method consists largely of listening to rote recitation of set passages and pointing out questions which have been asked about them in all previous exams. Mr. Devine lives in the basement flat below the home of Mrs. Dempsey, a respectable Catholic widow. His recreation consists of stage-managing amateur theatricals. The novel concerns Mr. Devine's romance with Una Clarke, a twenty-year old Protestant girl, the niece of Tim Heron, another lay master at St. Michan's.

Moore links Devine's romance to a struggle for power within the College. The ambitious Dean of Discipline, Father McSwiney, wishes to become President of St. Michan's, displacing from that office the aged Father Keogh. The Presidency of St. Michan's is the apex of a rigidly hierarchical and paternalistic social structure. The person who holds the office has absolute power over the staff as well as the students of the school. The book shows that authority in St. Michan's is spiritual in principle, but sadistic in practice. The dynamic of the school is the physical and mental suffering imposed on its members. The students are routinely flogged by the masters; in turn, the boys brutalize the smallest and weakest among themselves. The masters, particularly the lay masters, live in terror of clerical disapproval. In the intertwined stories of Devine's romance and Father McSwiney's ambition, Moore defines a conception of power and explores its consequences for the individual person.

At the opening of the book, Devine is what everyone in his world expects him to be. He is steady, solid, unfailingly reliable. He appears to be an adult acting responsibly in society; however like Judith Hearne, he is trapped in a prolonged childhood, a fact which the external circumstances of his life reveal. He is in daily contact with the relics of his dead parents. His flat in Mrs. Dempsey's basement is filled with their furniture and dominated by their wedding picture. He still sleeps in the bed of his boyhood. Like a good child, Devine is anxious to avoid trouble. He can be intimidated by bus conductors and church sextons. His inoffensiveness is reflected in the universal recognition of the fact that he is, as the Dean of Discipline remarks, "a harmless enough lad." (p. 97)

Devine's disastrous childishness, like Judith Hearne's, reveals itself when he attempts to achieve an adult sexual relationship. Up to his meeting with Una Clarke, his contacts with women have been few and humiliating. Still a virgin, he conducts his sexual life inside his head, always viewing such fantasizing as sin. In defense of his masculinity attacked in an overheard conversation, he reflects that he has as many sinful thoughts as any other man. But he does think, quite correctly, that his woman-less plight is somehow connected to the school in which he has lived as boy and man. "It was the education in Ireland, dammit, he had said it many a time. He had been a boarder at this very school, shut off from girls until he was almost a grown man." (p. 9)

From the first Dev's courtship of Una is conditioned by a double view of her which can be explained by his sexual naiveté and his cultural training. On the one hand, he sees her as innocent: "She was young and there was something wild and unfinished about her, as though she were in her first year of nylon stockings and lipstick and not yet used to them." (p. 42) At the same time he sees her as mysteriously worldly and sexually experienced because of her exotic Protestantism and her past involvement with a married man in Dublin. Ultimately Dev's decision to marry her is motivated by his own fear. When he mistakenly thinks that she is pregnant by the Dubliner, he decides to propose. He is certain that Una in her desperate predicament will not be able to turn him down. Moreover, he thinks that he need never face a sexual humiliation from her because she will always be indebted to him for saving her. Suspecting his own impotence, he can only find safety in a woman's weakness and degradation.

The evening of Dev's real proposal to Una is like the night of Judith Hearne's fancied proposal from Madden; it brings his life to its highest point of happiness, and it initiates the panic which leads to an immediate humiliation and to a future experience of absolute abasement. The proposal itself seems to go well, but the bright promise of the evening is shattered when, later the same night in Dev's flat, Una makes a sexual demand on him. The scene between them is the staple of a thousand jokes lived through in all its misery. The situation is managed to bring into sharp focus the destructive potential in both of them—the raw obtuseness of Una, her awkwardness and inexperience; Dev's fear and ignorance, his physical shame, his puritanism. No flicker of comedy alleviates the deadliness of the encounter of these two virgins.

Moore shows us that what torments Dev when he is alone with Una in the flat is a sense of the human body— hers, but most especially his own—as awkward, grotesque, shameful. In a real sexual situation with a woman for the first time in his life, he cannot reconcile his fantasies of romantic love with this sense of the repulsiveness of the body. Desperately he tries to move Una into his mind by associating her with the women of his fantasy life and with religion, but the living girl will not retreat into his mind. Intercourse in this real moment becomes for Dev a humiliating obscenity. Impotent and sick with terror, he runs from the bed in which Una is lying.

In tracing out the consequences for Dev of the night with Una, Moore explores the connection between Dev's inability to function sexually as an adult and the fact that he holds a child's place in the society in which he lives. His adult social role is seen to be a sham. Dev, like the students in his class, is a powerless and victimized boy. The extent of his helplessness becomes clear as he tries to protect himself from the consequences of spending the night alone with a woman. His only weapons are those of the terrified child: deceit and treachery. Repeatedly he lies to Tim Heron about having been with Una. In his fear, he abandons her to the wrath of her family by refusing to cooperate with her in devising a cover story that will involve him, and protect her. Over two days he nurtures a desperate hope that things will quiet down. But the situation is too complicated; he is overwhelmed.

The events of the final day of Dev's crisis make absolutely clear the link between the institutionalized sadism of St. Michan's and sexual repression, a link which is central to Moore's presentation of authority in the Belfast Catholic community. The day begins with Dev methodically flogging his way through his first class. In his second class of twelve boys:—"almost ready to shave, their faces ugly with the signs of adolescence . . . dangerous" (p. 212)—he asks a question about the setting of the opening scene of *Julius Caesar* on the Feast of Lupercal; four boys fail to answer and are waiting to be caned when Dev is called out of the room to speak to Una on the phone. Again he refuses to help her. He goes back to the classroom and is tormented by the conviction that the boys have been gossiping about him in his absence. He feels that his authority is broken, that his cane is useless. This moment in the classroom is the exact parallel of the sexual test with Una. Indeed the image in which two nights before in his bedroom he had foreseen his failure with her, predicted this scene in the schoolroom. In his thoughts as he walked "like a man condemned" to the bed was the schoolroom: "In sinful dreams he had seen himself as master, male, menacing. But now, he was sick as a boy who had not prepared: the role had been reversed, he was victim, he would be punished for his failure." (p. 149) In the actual schoolroom, his moral authority is being tested, and the occasion for the test is provided by a reference to sexual failure. He begins to read to the boys an explanatory note on the Lupercalia. When he reads that the priests of Lupercus beat with throngs barren women, someone laughs: "Some boy, among the twelve, had stifled a short obscene chuckle." (p. 215) He goes on reading and the boy laughs again. Dev looks at the inscrutable faces of his students and knows again his impotence: " . . . they were not listening. His private life was a dirty joke. They were not listening. He was no longer master." (p. 216)

Dev's failures in the bedroom and in the classroom are

interchangeable. He lacks the sexual and the moral
authority of a man; accordingly his role is to suffer
power as does a child—or a woman. Heron outraged
at Dev's belated attempt to defend Una and his confession of impotence, beats him with a master's cane until
both are sated. In this scene, Heron and Dev, as punisher
and victim, express the dynamic of all the relationships
in the book: master and student, father and child,
husband and wife.

Like Judith Hearne, Dev has modeled himself on
Christ as child and Christ as victim. In his flat, Dev
keeps two religious pictures from his father's house; one
is of the Divine Infant of Prague, the other, a print of
a seventeenth-century *Ecce Homo*. In combination the two
pictures represent the community ideal: the divine baby
in the robes of the priest embodies sexual innocence and
a purely spiritual conception of power; the thorn-
crowned, lacerated head, submission and obedience to
civic authority and to the will of the divine Father. As we
have seen, Judith Hearne's dual hallucination of herself
as Infant Christ and crucified Christ is the result of the
perfect internalization of these ideals. Dev's acceptance
of them is as complete as hers, though more subtly
expressed. Moore associates motifs of the passion and
death of Christ with moments when Dev's inability to
deal with situations as an adult is most pronounced.
For example, in his customary child's act of hiding and
spying—this time on some boys who are trying to wash
some scandalous graffiti about him from the wall of a
lavatory—he stands on the seat of a toilet and turns
himself into the corpus on the cross: "Arms outstretched,
trembling on tiptoe, he closed his eyes, letting his head

hang in relief." (p. 170) In the Lupercal scene, he is the master among twelve, one of whom is a public betrayer. In the bedroom scene, Dev prays, like Christ at the agony in the garden, that God spare him the impending trial. He feels himself shamefully stripped, walks to the bed like a condemned man, and reacts to Una's command to lie on top of her as if she were indeed his cross. At the end of the encounter, Una screams twice at him, "Oh, Christ." Dev's very name expresses his assimilation of the Christ-like ideal. No one calls him by his first name, Diarmuid; he is always addressed by his surname or its short form. Diarmuid is the lover of Finn's wife in the Irish sagas. In Dev, the passionate man is negated by the effort to deny his own humanity, to live as if he were sexless, bodiless—divine.

While the Christ-like Dev in his masochistic passivity fills the ideal of sonship, the aggressive and rebellious Father McSwiney—his name too is important—violates it. It is for this reason that Dev is protected by Father Keogh at the end of the book, and Father McSwiney is punished. Beneath their obvious differences in energy and assertiveness, Dev and the Dean are in the same condition; they are middleaged and celibate; their adult status in the school covers their real subservience to a complex network of men who are to them as fathers. The paternal principle is spiritual. It expresses itself in a series of increasingly abstract paternal relationships which stretch from the family to the clergy through the church hierarchy to the papacy and ultimately to God the Father. The refectory of St. Michan's expresses with precision the filial status of all its members. The students sit at trestle tables in "prison rows." The staff sits on a

platform above them, the clergy at one table in order
of rank, the laity at another in order of social class.
Above the platform are pictures of four Irish bishops.
Father Keogh, the President, has close ties with the
papacy, having spent years teaching in Rome. He
devotes himself, while administering the school, to an
appropriate scholarly project, "a record of Irish clerical
pilgrimages to the Vatican in the nineteenth century."
(p. 195)

The members of this community transform physical
paternity into a spiritual relation by envisioning sexual
intercourse as an act in which the male expresses moral
authority. This community conceptualizes intercourse in
terms of the Lupercal ritual, a fact which explains the
boy's obscene laughter and Dev's instant understanding of the significance of that laughter. Moore's Belfast
Catholics see copulation as corporal punishment
presided over by a priest. The cane and the phallus, as
we have seen, are identical. The punitive dimension
abstracts and spiritualizes the sex act; intercourse is the
expression of moral force rather than of natural gener-
ative love.

The paternal principle abstracted into a series of ever
more symbolic relationships forms a structure for experience; the alternative to that structure is chaos, annihila-
tion. At the end of the book, when the President not
only keeps Devine in his job, but tolerates his feeble
statement of defiance, Dev sees that the old man has
saved him: "He had thrown himself off the cliff; but by
some miracle, he was still hanging to a rock on the cliff
face. The President was the rock." (p. 235) The image in
which Dev envisions Father Keogh's action toward him
shows that he sees it as protection from the terrors of

chaotic space. Dev's real father, though dead for four-teen years, offers the same protection. Dev has a memory of his reaction as a ten year old watching his father swim out to sea: "He had wept—his daddy was swimming away forever! To Scotland. . . . " (p. 13) The desperate fear of abandonment to the wide world without paternal protection survives in Dev's habit of turning his father's signet ring in every situation of stress. Through the compulsive gesture of his son, the elder Devine becomes a ghostly presence in the book.

Dev's childlikeness, like that of Judith Hearne, is shown to be contemptible, and contemptible for the same reason. He too has withdrawn from the community into the isolated world of fantasy. At the end of the book, caught forever in the bondage of childhood, he understands that his failure with Una is the decisive act of his life; he also understands that the fantasies on which he has always lived, which have sustained him till his middle age in the hope for a fulfilled life, have insured his impotence. As he moves through the crisis over Una, he thinks again and again that he is not potent because he has removed sex from the world of reality to the inner world of fantasy and daydream. In the desperate moments before Una comes to his bed, he understands that for him physical desire is absolutely removed from the real world: "Desire was a mental lusting, a making of improbable dreams." (p. 147) Seeing Una asleep after the scene in the bedroom, he is moved by desire for her and imagines raping her: "Was that not his sinful imagination once more, the imagination which atrophied reality? No, he could not, he would feel only shame and terror if those eyes opened, if she accepted, if she waited for him to make love." (p. 151) To approach sex as a human interchange between two persons, to accept without hierarchical sanctions the real body of a real woman in the actual moment, is to accept the weight and significance of the world in which men live. Dev is no more able to make this act of acceptance than any other member of the community. He differs from others only in working out the consequences of this inhuman denial in endless masturbatory fantasies. The functioning members of the community work it out by institutionalizing sadism. Heron and Father McSwiney, unlike Dev, are at one with their society: one is a married man, the other a priest; both are sadists.

The imagination is Dev's retreat not only from sex but also from the sense of his own mortality. In a solitary interlude between his humiliation in the classroom and his flogging by Heron, he sees that he has hidden in daydream from "moments . . . when a life hereafter does not seem believable, when heaven and hell are only words without meaning, matched against the fact of the breathing stopped, the heart stilled." (p. 217) In the withdrawal inward to fantasy, Dev has done what the community does by religion— he has escaped the generational realities of sex and death; he has denied his humanity and the significance of the daily actualities of his life. The imagination in this book, as in Moore's first, merely isolates; it does not liberate from the life-denying abstractions of the community ideal. In Moore's Belfast, there is no Stephen Dedalus. The spinster alcoholic and the impotent bachelor who once thought of himself as the Irish Baudelaire lack the intelligence of Stephen Dedalus, but more crucially his power and his sense of the overriding validity of the life of the imagination.

2

The Guilt of the Novelist

Of *The Luck of Ginger Coffey* (Boston, 1960), Moore has said: "I tried to mix three styles in this novel: realistic style, comedy, and tragedy, and to do something that actually could happen realistically in certain scenes in the book in a farcical way. To lift it out of flat realism." (See Robert Fulford, "Brian Moore," *Tamarack Review,* Spring, 1962, p. 14.) He goes on to discuss the courtroom episode at the end of the book as an example of this mixed style, that is as a scene whose realistic details are impeccably correct. "But it's done almost in play-form and it reads, I think, almost as a piece of farce which has no relation to truth." I suggest that the change to which Moore is referring by means of these concepts of mixed styles and of submerged material is the fact that with this book the symbolic function of the apparently realistic fiction in relation to Moore himself as artist has become a significant element in the novel itself. Not only in isolated scenes is it possible to see something beneath Moore's realism, but in the novel as a whole. The realistic surface of *The Luck of Ginger Coffey* remains opaque unless we view the book in relation to the recurring concerns of Moore's fiction and in relation to the essential biographical fact that

35

Moore made a reputation for himself as a serious novelist with two books that were written in Canada about life in Belfast. The relation of the failure Coffey to the successful writer Moore is the source of the novel's complexity and interest.

This third novel confronts the vision of the desirable life implied in the Belfast books. Judith Hearne and Devine suffer from confinement within a paternalist system; Coffey is free—of dominating parents, of Catholicism, even of Ireland itself. But Coffey's freedom carries its own punishment. His fictional predecessors are trapped in too little space; he is lost in too much. Dev and Judith Hearne hold traditionally defined and changeless places in society, but Coffey sees his social identity dissolve around him. He has broken his tie to Ireland, but has not formed one to Canada. Abruptly he finds himself outside the bourgeois world he has always inhabited. His marriage disintegrates; no longer husband and father, he is suddenly rootless and solitary.

He is stateless, classless, homeless; his plight is the exact reverse of that of the Belfast characters, but his suffering has the same cause, or rather, he is punished for the same crime. Coffey, like Judith Hearne and Devine before him, lives too much in his fantasies. Where they dreamed of love, Coffey dreams of adventure. The journey to Canada in 1955 is the heroic search for what he calls fame and fortune, the alternative to more desirable feats: " ... paddling down the Amazon with four Indian companions, climbing a peak in Tibet or sailing a raft from Galway to the West Indies." (p. 13) Coffey's emigration to Canada, like the love affairs in the Belfast novels, is the actualization by a person in middle age of a fantasy which is deeply cherished and supremely naive. Coffey's dreams of exploration and achievement, no less than Judith Hearne's of domestic bliss and Devine's of sexual triumph, are those of the superannuated child.

The retention of childhood in the Belfast novels is shown to be both the personal defect of the characters, locked in solipsistic dream, and the result of the pressure of the authority exerted by a paternalist society upon the individual person. In the creation of Coffey, Moore drops the emphasis on the social cause for the retained childhood and concentrates on the guilt attached to the self-enclosed life of the imagination. This movement away from a social explanation for the failure to grow up explains the Irish background which Moore creates for Coffey. Unlike Devine and Judith Hearne in British Ulster, Coffey, a Dubliner born in 1916, is historically a new kind of Irishman, the citizen of an autonomous country. The paternalist institutions in the new Ireland continue to function, but they are benign at best, annoying at worst. Coffey has no trouble with family. From his rare thoughts about them, we learn that his solicitor father was buried in a Franciscan habit, having left Coffey the two-thousand pound legacy which made possible the journey to Canada. In Coffey's experience, the church admonishes but does not overwhelm. The fifteen-year-old Ginger heard a retreat sermon which exhorted the boys at Plunkett School to give up dreams of foreign adventure and stay home in Ireland, a light demand when one considers those made on Stephen Dedalus forty years before, and on the parishioners of St. Finbar's in Belfast twenty-five years later.

The journey to Canada was an act of treachery. Oppressed by no force, in pursuit of his private fantasy, Coffey in one stroke betrayed Ireland, the family, and the church, since he used the money inherited from his father to leave his native land against the explicit command of the church and the tacit demand of society. In Canada for the first few months, however, Coffey retained his link with Ireland in the form of the untouched money for the return passage. In using the passage money, he reinforces the original betrayal, and when the money is gone, Coffey finds himself not only without his link to Ireland, but also without class location and without family. The book begins at the point of disintegration in Coffey's life; the action of the novel is his attempt to reestablish order, to regain social identity, to restore the lost family.

In the service of these goals, Coffey takes simultaneously two menial jobs, one of them as a nonunion proofreader for a newspaper, one as route-man for a diaper service. As a penniless foreigner doing despised work, he is forced into a radical confrontation with a world which is absolutely alien to him. Yet the two jobs in this new world offer Coffey the old Irish choice between accepting actuality and retreating from it, and Coffey makes the old Irish mistake in choosing the latter alternative. A diaper service is indeed hostile to romance; accordingly in his work at Tiny Ones, Coffey becomes free of old illusions. But at the newspaper, eminently susceptible to romance, he ensnares himself in new ones. Perversely, it is only the job at the *Tribune* that matters to him.

At Tiny Ones, Coffey confronts a major fantasy of his past and releases himself from it. In pursuit of adventure, Coffey had joined the Irish Army in 1939. He served bitterly until 1945, deprived of his dream of war by Ireland's neutrality and by his wife, who opposed his plan to leave her and the infant Paulie and desert to England. "He wanted to see some action but she said his duty was with his family. Family! He wanted adventure, not diapers." (p. 29) Ever since the war, Coffey has affected the style and bluff heartiness of the veteran British officer. At Tiny Ones, willing to settle now for diapers, he meets Mr. Stanley Mountain, who runs the truck depot as a military post. Coffey dons the pseudo-military uniform of the company—whose insignia is Winston Churchill, "neatly diapered"—and remembers "the first time he had worn a uniform, as a private in the Regiment of Pearse; still a boy, still dreaming of wars, battles and decorations." (p. 114) Under the banner of Churchill at last as "a regular member of the shit brigade," (p. 115) Coffey gains from Tiny Ones in ironic and concentrated form what he might have achieved if he had in 1941 managed to join the British Army—introduction to the irreducible physical reality of common human experience and a true liberation from the obsessive parochialism of Irish life.

On Tiny Ones business, Coffey enters the apartment of an old Dublin acquaintance, and a most significant one, since she summons up a large part of Coffey's Irish past: "Colonel Kerrigan's daughter, the same girl he had danced with last winter at the Plunkett Old Boys' Dance in the Shelbourne Hotel. And had served under her old man in the Army." (p. 131) Unsuccessfully, he tries to conceal his identity under a false name, and he leaves the apartment shamed and envisioning all of Ireland laughing at the story that will be told in "Gath and embroidered in the Wicklow Lounge."

> Ha, ha! cried all the contrified young thicks he had gone to school with, who now, ordained and Roman-collared, regularly lectured the laity on politics and love. Ha, ha! cried the politicians, North and South, united as always in fostering that ignorance which alone made possible their separate powers. Hah! cried the archbishops, raising their purple skull-capped heads from the endless composition of pastoral letters on the dangers of foreign dances and summer frocks. Hah! cried the smug old businessmen, proud of being far behind the times. Ha, ha, ha! Emigrate, would you? *We told you so.* (p. 132–133)

The distribution of laughters here—two parts clergy to one part politician and one part businessman—constitutes the power structure in Irish society. At the moment when Ginger feels his humiliation before all Ireland, Moore presents his commitment to Canada, using the words of the marriage ceremony: "And in that moment he knew that, sink or swim, Canada was home now, for better or for worse, for richer or for poorer, until death." (p. 133) Service in the shit brigade has given Coffey a new national identity.

It is through the newspaper job, however, that Coffey wants to restore his class status and his marriage. He sees the tedious work he does on the paper as preparation for the far more glamorous work of a reporter. In the service of this illusion and against all rational evidence, Coffey submits himself to the domination of

MacGregor, the paper's managing editor, who is a composite of the priests in the Belfast novels. He is thin, elderly, furious—a petty dictator terrorizing those under his authority. MacGregor is persistently associated with Catholicism and with God the Father. At his right hand, MacGregor is constantly attended by one Clarence, ever ready to carry out commands. The counterpart of the pair is made explicit: " . . . MacGregor appeared, Jehovah at the far end of the corridor, attended by Clarence, his fat ministering angel." (p. 191) MacGregor is, in fact, well placed in a secular hierarchy, which serves the Canadian god, who is clearly identified by Fox, Coffey's fellow-proofreader: "Money is the root of all good here," he says to Coffey of Canada. "One nation, indivisible, under Mammon that's our heritage." (p. 70) MacGregor, tyrant over reporters and proofreaders, is himself subject to his publisher, a Mr. Hound, who is well named since he is in fact the hound of Mammon's heaven. Fox points out that the newspaper functions in the service of power and money; its only real interest is in advertising. MacGregor is a prelate in a secular religion in which power is dependent on money rather than on spiritual authority. The Canadian counterpart of the Irish power structure is provided by the ten rich men, "Ten big finenceers," (p. 71) who run the country. Moore presents money in Canada as an abstractly paternal ordering force, like religion in the Belfast books; it is dehumanized power hierarchically administered.

Tiny Ones and A.K. Brott, its owner, offer an alternative to MacGregor and the religion of Mammon, an alternative which does not exist in the Belfast books and which justifies Coffey's pledge of fidelity to Canada. Money at Tiny Ones is a manageable and human commodity; the hierarchy which dispenses it does not disappear out of sight. It begins with the humane Corp, goes on to the preposterous Mr. Mountain, and ends at the top with Brott. Brott's office, the inmost citadel of Tiny Ones power is decorated with "photographs in black frames, ex-voto scenes from the life of A.K. Brott." (p. 135) The language of religion here points up Brott's human vanity, not his divinity, and the pictures show him as a man in a variety of human and personal relationships. When Brott offers Coffey the job as his personal assistant, he remarks on the corruption of the Mammon-serving press: "Never saw a reporter in this province you couldn't buy off for twenty bucks in a plain envelope." (p. 198)

Brott's offer is Coffey's chance to regain his wife at the price of renouncing his dream of success in Canada. Coffey, however, does not want his wife back under that condition. Again and again, Coffey asks of himself and of others the question he asks of Brott when the job offer is made: "What do you think I came to this country for?" (p. 199) In truth, Coffey came to Canada to transform himself into a successful and powerful man, to escape his Irish role of subservience and failure. Coffey refuses Brott because he wants to keep his wife and to transform himself, but the substructure of the fiction is ordered to show that the change Coffey desires involves a horrifying loss of his past and of the identity which the past has conferred upon him.

The Coffey marriage is the metaphor for the bond between the displaced Irishman and his native land.

Veronica Coffey's maiden name—Shannon—ties her to the very landscape of Ireland. Coffey in his most tender reflections about Veronica calls her by one of the names for Ireland, Dark Rosaleen. She wears the wedding ring of Coffey's mother and clings to the values of Irish Catholicism, although she no longer practices them. She is hostile to Coffey's love for Paulie, the Irish born child whose future is clearly Canadian, another indication that she is the jealous past. Veronica is the recalcitrant substance of the Irish world that Coffey in coming to Canada sought to escape. At the same time, Coffey clings to her because she defines him.

The Canadian present and the Irish past can be reconciled only by Coffey's failure in Canada. If he takes the humiliating job at Tiny Ones, he can retain Veronica and stay in Canada. At the end of the book, Coffey makes that capitulation, but Moore works out the alternative to it in his presentation of the struggle between Coffey and Gerry Grosvenor for Veronica. The question of which of them is to have Veronica is very deeply the question of who Coffey is going to be in Canada, and of how the Irish past is going to survive for him. Grosvenor is presented in the book with a limited but important set of attributes. His first appearance is marked by the observation that "adolescence, like an incurable disease, had never quite left him." (p. 30) He is a successful cartoonist, who drinks too much and lives alone. The few things we know about Grosvenor link him to Coffey: he is immature; as artist and drunk, he is isolated in the private world of the imagination. Grosvenor with his English name, his Canadian

nationality, his anti-Catholicism, his hostility to
Ireland, projects a version of Coffey as successful and
deracinated.

Moore links Grosvenor to a second reflector of
Coffey, the arch-solipsist Warren K. Wilson, whom
Coffey meets under very significant circumstances on the
day after Veronica leaves him. Alone in his room at the
YMCA Coffey hears on a distant radio the sound of a
woman singing a banal love song. He projects a future
for himself as hermit and saint, staying in the room till
death, never speaking, hearing only the voice of the
woman on the radio. He sees the woman as ageless,
immune to time, indifferent to death; she is in fact a
vulgar cousin of the girl who sang at Key West in one
of the most famous poems of Wallace Stevens, a poet
whose work gives one of Moore's novels its title and
provides the epigraph for another. The singing woman
presides over Coffey's inner world, as Veronica presides
over his outer world. When Coffey abruptly realizes
that his satisfaction in the role of saint depends on an
outside spectator perceiving him play it, he renounces
the woman and trying to still her voice, stumbles into
the pitch-black room in which Wilson, garbed only in
underpants and wearing the radio around his neck is
busy developing pictures in pursuit of his ambition to
become a world famous photographer of movie stars.
Wilson lives alone in constantly changing rented rooms,
pathetically busy at the succession of mail-order courses
which are intended to lead him to the fulfillment of his
dream. He has no roots in any place and no human
connections. Sex is merely a problem solved with brutal

simplicity: "Any time I feel like it, I just check into a hotel, buy a quart of liquor and ask the bellboy to send a pig up." (p. 110) During his separation from Veronica, Coffey is tormented by a recurring fantasy in which a whorish Veronica abandons herself to Grosvenor, who appears to Coffey with the face of Wilson. The implications of this fantasy do not become apparent until Grosvenor sends Coffey to the rendezvous with the prostitute who is to supply the false evidence of adultery which will end the Coffey marriage. The prostitute's name is Melody Ward; she is the singing woman materialized. If Coffey had followed Melody Ward into the hotel room, he would have given Veronica to Gerry Grosvenor, that is prostituted his past by disconnecting himself from it as an actuality, and moving it into his imagination. The site of the proposed transfer is a seedy hotel called by the name of MacGregor's faithful servant, the Clarence; the internalization of the past is to take place under the auspices of the god Clarence serves. Veronica internalized by Coffey would become Melody Ward and preside over Coffey's private and exploitable fictive world. We have already seen the unlovely vision of the pair: Wilson the aged baby laboring in the dark room for fame with the woman singing from the radio hanging around his neck.

The same desirable and unthinkable transformations of Coffey into Grosvenor and Veronica into Melody Ward lie behind the allegedly sacrificial bargain that Coffey makes with Veronica in which he promises to end the marriage and give her to Grosvenor if MacGregor does not promote him to reporter by a given day. With this bargain Coffey joins the heroes of the Belfast books in casting himself in the role of Christ, though unlike them, he assumes the role consciously. But Coffey is not so much sacrificing himself as the identity which the past has given him. There is no difference in terms of the underlying dynamic of the book between the two possible results of Coffey's gamble; if he wins by becoming J.F. Coffey, journalist, he becomes the Canadian success, that is Grosvenor. If he loses, he gives Veronica—his past—to Grosvenor. The alternatives are interchangeable.

Grosvenor and Wilson as a pair reveal the identity Coffey might build for himself in Canada if he breaks his real bond to Ireland. Billy Davis and Fox are also reflectors of Coffey whom Moore uses to show that Coffey can never escape the Irish past or the ultimate truth of his own weakness. On the crucial day on which MacGregor denies Coffey the promotion, Moore presents Coffey in encounters with both Billy Davis and Fox. At Coffey's very first meeting with Davis, Moore establishes an association between them by Davis's appearance, which is a parody of Coffey's, a fact that Coffey does not notice, though he does think that Davis looks like Uncle Sam. (p. 68) At their final meeting, Coffey learns with a shock that Davis is Irish born and that he came to Canada in pursuit of success: "I'm an immigrant, same as you. Donegal man, born and bred. Came out here when I was twenty years old, looking for the streets that were paved with gold." (p. 205) Davis looks like Uncle Sam and speaks without accent, but tattooed on his skin are the signs of his past attachment to Ireland and to a lost woman named Min, a word that summons another—"mine." Davis separated himself from Ireland and lost everything. He is a failed and abandoned old man, condemned to die in the center of a foreign city in loneliness and poverty. The renunciation of Irish identity and the allegiance to Mammon can lead to nothing but desolating loss. The deracinated Irishman cannot graft himself into a new national life; he can only wither and die.

Fox is the reflector who reveals Coffey with the most terrifying finality. On his first appearance in the book, Fox is shown to be intelligent, cynical, and crippled. The link which ties him to Coffey is his crutch, for Coffey identifies himself with the victim in the Cripple-Mate Case, the sensational murder of a cripple by his wife and her lover. In the final encounter between the two men in the all-night diner of the hugely maternal Rose Alma Briggs, Fox reveals what always remains hidden in Coffey: his contempt for the vulgarity of Canadian materialism and his sense of Canada's inability to generate national feeling in her citizens. More deeply he reveals Coffey's savage egotism. Fox's past as alcoholic vagrant indicates his enclosure in fantasy. Coffey, drunk on Fox's wine, tries to flee from him, but Fox attacks with wine bottle and crutch. Coffey, who regularly beats Grosvenor because he must defeat the image of himself as successful and Canadian, is immobilized by Fox waving the symbols of Coffey's own weakness and addiction to fantasy. "Cruel cripple doomsayer!" (p. 215) thinks Coffey, as he tries to attack Fox. Brutal, maimed, locked in fantasy and in failure, Fox is the hidden core of Coffey's being.

Coffey is protected from Fox by Rose Alma, whom Fox calls "Rose of the World." The reference to Yeats's poem and her benign motherliness suggest that she too is associated with the Irish past which gave Coffey his identity. Rose Alma looks at Coffey and compassionately recognizes "his true face," that of a lost boy. (p. 217) She sends him home to wife and daughter, but before he can reach them, he must be punished for his ambitions and his fantasies. Like Devine and Judith Hearne, he finds his crucifixion in a scene of absolute humiliation. Moore unites Christ and child once more as Coffey suffers for the child's act of urinating in public. His arrest and imprisonment are threaded with images of the passion of Christ. Having suffered sadistic punishments in jail and the child's sense of entrapment in a tight space, Coffey assumes responsibility for his sins, as Judith Hearne and Devine did before him in similar circumstances. In the courtroom of a judge whose first name is Amédée, and who sits under a crucifix, Coffey tries to protect his wife and child by assuming a false name: Gerald MacGregor. In choosing that name, Coffey unwittingly reveals his real crime—the betrayal involved in his attempts to claim MacGregor's god and Grosvenor's identity.

Moore presents Coffey's courtroom experience as crucially enlightening because in it Coffey moves outside his own subjectivity when he sees that to the spectators at his trial, he is merely a comic object. He understands that only to Veronica, who unites his disgraced present to his past in her loving perception, is he more than object. In acknowledging that he must be seen by a loving observer in order to exist continuously as person, he realizes the ultimate flaw in the solipsist's dedication to his own life of fantasy. The restoration of the Coffey marriage follows the trial and is consistent with the revelations about Coffey made by means of Billy Davis and Fox. The Irish past cannot be lost; Coffey's identity as incompetent and failure is immutably fixed. Coffey will have Veronica, though he no longer even wants her, and he will take the ludicrous and degrading job as executive assistant at Tiny Ones.

Moore said to Robert Fulford that Coffey "represents what I was terrified would happen to me. I've always felt myself to be a misfit, I still do." It would perhaps be more accurate to say that in terms of the stern morality which drives Moore's impulse to create fiction, Coffey represents what should have happened to Moore. Coffey is a character in a coherent and embodied fantasy who gets the fate which his creator at a deep and irrational level believes that the fantasizer deserves.

In *An Answer From Limbo* (Boston, 1962), Moore explores all the aspects of the struggle between his condemnation of the fantasizer and his own career as a successful novelist. Beneath the realistic surface of this novel, as in *The Luck of Ginger Coffey*, lies a demonstrably coherent symbolic pattern which is concerned with the activity of the novelist himself. The underpattern in the Canadian book conveys its author's guilt at his successful exploitation of his Irish past.

The underpattern in *An Answer From Limbo* ties authorial guilt to complicated aggressive forces which are felt to impel the creation of fiction. The figure of the fantasizer appears here at last in the shape in which its relation to Moore is unmistakable, that is as the Ulster-born novelist Brendan Tierney. The facts of Tierney's life are not precisely the facts of Moore's, but Tierney represents Moore as he conceives himself in the role of novelist.

In this book, Moore conveys the conflict between the fictive world which the fantasizer invents and the actual world in which he lives, by the juxtaposition of two narrative viewpoints. Brendan Tierney reveals himself in the first person. He addresses the reader quite directly, sharing his worries about the novel he is writing, exploring the ambitions which drive him, considering the effect of family problems on his ability to work. Brendan also appears with all the other characters in a narrative unfolded from a third-person omniscient perspective. The subject of the third-person narrative is the disintegration of Brendan's marriage and the abandonment and eventual death of his mother. In the economy established by Moore's narrative technique, the creation of Brendan's fictional world demands the destruction of his actual world.

The idea that writing a novel is an act of destruction is implicit in the way in which Moore varies the narrative perspective within the structure of the book, and it is an explicit element in Brendan's thinking about his art. In his first address to the reader, Brendan presents the memory of the event by which his commitment to art was made irrevocable. The schoolmates of the fourteen-year-old Brendan held him under a fountain as punishment for an essay he wrote in which he presented himself in the future: "I wrote that I would become a great poet, that I would devote my life to the composition of a masterpiece and that, at the age of thirty, coughing blood in a last consumptive frenzy, I hoped to die, my gift still clear and unmuddied." (p. 5) After the dunking, Brendan vanquished the gang by the undiminished force of his assertion that he would become a writer. Fifteen years later, the adult Brendan, now approaching the age of his sacrificial death for art, still sees fiction as a weapon. Regularly he reflects on the aggression-revenge motive for his writing. The desire to be a novelist is the desire "to revenge myself on the past by transforming it into a world of words." (p. 60) He sees himself as artist in the persona of Macbeth. (p. 50, p. 89)

This linking of punitive aggression and literary creation should be related to the linking in *The Feast of Lupercal* of sadistic punishment and sexual intercourse. Indeed Brendan's fountain memory insistently summons the chilly ambiance of St. Michan's. In both these books, Moore uses man's sexual punishment of woman as the paradigm for all expressions of power. All creation—physical, cosmic, aesthetic—involves the punitive exercise of masculine energy. In *An Answer From Limbo,* spirit is persistently associated with the male. Aesthetic and actual fathers fade into God, as does the hierarchy of fathers at St. Michan's in *The Feast of Lupercal.* Mrs. Tierney in her judgement dreams sees her own father in the role of God the father; Brendan in writing his book becomes an omnipotent creator. Women, on the other hand, are shown to be rawly corporeal, inviting and obscurely deserving the punishment they receive. The omniscient perspective gives the suffering and death of Mrs. Tierney and the sexual degradation of Jane the weight of inevitability. When Brendan withdraws from them, they are abandoned to a fearful punishment which the linking of events in the narrative suggests comes to them from an all-knowing, unforgiving, brutally sadistic God.

Both women are shown to be guilty of adulterous desires. Mrs. Tierney once at a family picnic almost seduced her husband's seminarian cousin. As an old woman in New York, she remembers through a dream the day almost forty years before when she allowed her "rucked-up" skirt to expose her bare thigh in order to arouse the cousin. Only a rain shower, which she correctly sees as providential, stopped the pair from intercourse. Of Jane Tierney, the very first thing we learn from the omniscient narrator is that she "dreamed of dark ravishers, young and fierce, who loomed in her thoughts like menacing yet exciting phalli." (p. 22) Jane is bored with the sexual practices of her husband; she wants to be "humiliated, robbed, degraded, defiled." (p. 22) Mrs. Tierney is punished for her day on the beach by an agonized death. Jane is punished for her perverse desire by an affair with Vito Italiano.

The structure and interrelation of the events which lead to Mrs. Tierney's death show that she is driven out of Brendan's house to die in punishment for that offence on the beach. Jane makes it impossible for her to stay with the family when she learns that Mrs. Tierney baptized the children, but the reader knows that an element motivating the baptism was Mrs. Tierney's sense of guilt. (p. 85, p. 174) Moreover Lisa reveals the baptisms of herself and Liam to Jane because the three are caught in a rainstorm, and the drops of water remind the child of the baptismal ritual. They remind the reader, however, of the rain on the beach at Portstewart. The seductively rucked-up skirt of the day at the beach is cruelly expiated as Mrs. Tierney lies on the floor of Frank Finnerty's apartment. In the only extended italicized passage in the book, the omniscient narrator, made more distant and dispassionate by the typographical device, describes the posture of her suffering:

> *She lay . . . on her left side, her arms raised as though she had been shot down in the act of putting her hands up. She had moved her head clear of the vomit on the rug and her face rested on the floor boards. Her hair fell over her eyes, her nightdress was rucked up, baring her buttocks and lower abdomen.* (p. 270)

Jane's punishment is a variant of Mrs. Tierney's. Vito strikes her to the floor as brutally as the unknown force strikes down Mrs. Tierney in the apartment. He begins his first assault on Jane with the remark that she has a mind like a sewer, (p. 166) a statement which echoes a comment Mrs. Tierney seems to have heard from her husband in response to a question she once asked about brothels. (p. 14, p. 213) There is something uncanny in the way in which Vito so perfectly embodies the dark ravisher of Jane's fantasy. In fact, his name marks him as an instrument of paternalist masculine power, the first name clearly meaning life, the surname calling up papal Italy, which Moore identified in *The*

Feast of Lupercal as the place where human paternal power
at its most abstract, draws its sanction from the
divine father. It is not surprising that Jane sees the
Pope's picture among the family photographs in the
Italiano parlor.

The sexuality of women is not only adulterous, but
it is tainted by its association with anality as the
grotesque display of Mrs. Tierney's lower body shows.
Jane drives the old woman out of the house with an
excremental epithet. (p. 227) Jane herself thinks of the
bathroom as her special domain, retiring to it at every
crisis, once inviting Brendan to make love to her there.
Moreover, her masochism is linked to a desire for more
exotic penetrations than Brendan will attempt. The
combination of lust and anality in women not only
degrades them, but associates their maternity with
excretion. The description of Mrs. Tierney's lower
body is anticipated in Jane's view of Mrs. Italiano,
who is safely asleep: "there in a double bed . . . , night-
dress rucked up over heavy veiny hips, yellowish-gray
hair spread like sea wrack across the bolster, an old woman who snored, twitched in the heat, moved a varicosed
ankle across the expanse of bedsheet." (p. 241) Moments
after seeing his mother, Jane watches the naked Vito
approach to take her and thinks of his mother's maternity: "she . . . saw in her mind's eye those heavy veiny
old thighs which bore this brutality into life." (p. 243)
The hips actually seen become the thighs associated
with child birth. The switch seems due not to a pecu-
liarity of Jane, but to the pattern operating in the
book which associates birth with excretion.

The structure of events in the third person narrative

implies that women can be protected from divine sadistic energy only by the love of the men who have proper authority over them within the family system. Mrs. Tierney is safe from the final punishment so long as her husband is alive, and would have been safe till her own death if Brendan had loved her. Jane is safe from the consequences of her masochistic fantasies so long as Brendan is interested in their marriage. Mrs. Tierney alone in her death agony begs her husband, her dead eldest son, and Brendan for help, and then in her last thought cries to the nameless watcher of her suffering: *"Love me?"* (p. 290) Hours later, Jane in despair looks down over an infernal New York and asks the reverse of Mrs. Tierney's question: "Who do I love?" (p. 308) and must answer that she loves no one. Neither woman would have been driven to those sad and desperate questions if Brendan had retained his place in the generational world.

Yet the generational world is a horrifying one. Though human love within marriage and the family mitigates its brutality, its essential processes are inseparable from masculine cruelty and feminine degradation. Vito Italiano, punitive ravisher of Jane and protector of his widowed mother, is man operating in the generational order. In his account of the fountain incident, Brendan traces his original retreat from this world to a sense of incapacity, inability to assume his place in it: "As a child I feared that I was stupid and cowardly and thought that I would be a disappointment to all who knew me. I read a great deal and like many unsure children I had a taste for tragic endings." (p. 4) The image he presented to his schoolmates of himself as a dying poet came out of the escape reading of his childhood and combined two elements: first the dazzling purity of the poet's creative power, which is compared to a pure stream, second the weakness and passivity of the poet as victim of incurable disease. The dunking in the fountain by the schoolboys which follows the public revelation of this fantasy-self is the revenge of the community on the weak man; what the boys did to Brendan is the parallel of what Heron did to Devine. In both cases the man who has confessed to weakness is treated as a woman by the sadistic male community. The dunking in the fountain is a masculine ceremony of possession and cleansing—a baptism and a violation. It is the essential act of power.

Moore's presentation of the fountain incident in *An Answer From Limbo* both reveals and conceals its importance. On the one hand, Brendan as first person narrator traces his commitment to art to that event at the school. On the other, the wry tone of Brendan's reflection on his Belfast past makes the memory seem to be simply a bitterly funny anecdote about the woes of adolescence. A story which Moore published in 1961 (*Midstream*, Winter), presents the fountain memory in almost identical form, but this time it carries an unmistakable sense of outrage. "Preliminary Pages for a Work of Revenge" is clearly a preliminary to *An Answer From Limbo*. The story has no narrative element; it is a direct expression of anger and guilt, a warning that people will be hurt by the book it promises, and finally a direct plea for love. *An Answer From Limbo* clothes the complex emotions so harshly displayed in the story. But the relation of novel to story reveals very clearly the creative dynamic which drives Moore as an artist and which constitutes the real subject of *An Answer From Limbo*.

The story is built on the pattern of the introductory material to a book; within the pattern a raging first-person author-narrator addresses a hated reader. The story begins with a reversal of the traditional formula about the relation of fiction and reality: "*The characters in this work are meant to be real. References to persons living and dead are intended.*" In the section called "Acknowledgments" the author writes that he is grateful to no one, although he admits that "relatives and friends, enemies and acquaintances" have unwittingly given him material of which he will make personal and impressionistic use in his fiction. He compares himself to Pilate in knowing "only that truth is not the accurate rendition of facts." The longest section, "About the Author," makes an attempt in the beginning to present the reader as universal persecutor and the author as universal victim: "I am that person you insulted. I am that person you forgot. I am the one you do not speak of, the person you hope never to meet again." The reproach loses its general reference and focuses on a betraying wife or mistress. Then the narrator turns to accuse his classmates and presents the fountain incident in a form substantially identical to that in *An Answer From Limbo* except that the schoolmates are addressed in the second person.

In the novel, the fountain scene ends with Brendan reflecting that he has not yet become great, though he has published six stories in small literary magazines: "Yet the novel with which I hope to fulfill my prophesy lies in a drawer in my office, a loved but ailing child, its life endangered by my fitful labors." (p. 6) The ending of the incident in the story, addressed to the schoolmates, is savage:

> ... I did not become great. I had no vocation for great-ness. At thirty instead of coughing blood, I bled rectally from haemorrhoids. I who boasted to you that I would never settle for the ordinary avocations you proposed have settled instead for failure. Yet in writing this I show that I have not even the dignity of the man who has accepted a fate, no matter how despicable. I am still unable to agree to my failure because on the day, when by your fear you gave me a taste of what greatness might bring me, my course was set suddenly, haphazardly, yet with no possible alter-native routing, towards a destiny I was not fit to accomplish.

Where *An Answer From Limbo* gives us the artist struggling to create by imaginative effort the book for which the proper metaphor is the loved child, the story in the exact position of the book-as-child reference presents the rectal bleeding of the narrator as a sign of his failure as an artist.

In the concluding paragraphs of the story, the nar-rator's rage abruptly disappears. He accuses himself of being his own Judas in writing the very words we are reading, for in so writing he has turned away from the creation of the work "terrible in its truth" by which he could both redeem himself and revenge himself. He wonders what the truth is that he seeks to write, who it is on whom he must revenge himself, if he really is the victim of others. He reduces all his accusations to one mild one: "I can only say now that long ago your unwillingness to let me dream prevented for years my true awakening." Then he addresses a reader whose identity seems to be singular and specific, and concludes the story that began as a display of his hatred with a plea to that person for recognition and love.

The identification between the narrator of this story and the intelligence shaping it is clear. The title of the story, its content, and the textual repetitions make equally clear the fact that the narrator of the story and the writer of *An Answer From Limbo* are one and the same. Within *An Answer From Limbo,* however, the crucial relationship between Brian Moore as author and Brendan Tierney as character is never made clear. The result of that obscurity is a serious difficulty in understanding the death of Mrs. Tierney. That death is a very complex matter in terms of this book in itself and as the reversal of significant patterns which we have seen in the earlier books. The agonized dying of the mother, like Judith Hearne's moment before the tabernacle and Devine's beating by Heron, is the most painful and powerful action presented in the narrative. The short story directs us to read *An Answer From Limbo* as an act of revenge. I would suggest that the presentation of the death is the very core of that act. The revenge consists of the demonstration to those who have humiliated the novelist, of his immense power, the godlike power of the creator. We have argued that the punishment of the maternal body by the powerful father functions for Moore as the primary creative act. The sadism of the father is the universal fact of creation. In the book Mrs. Tierney is punished at the will of the novelist who has created her; the issue of her suffering is the very book in which she suffers, Brendan's book, which is *An Answer From Limbo*.

The identification of Moore's book with Brendan's is obscured but not obliterated. *An Answer From Limbo* contains two specific references to the content of Brendan's novel; both concern childbirth. There are no scenes of childbirth in *An Answer From Limbo;* however the book itself is about its own birth and the birth of Brendan as a writer. The first reference to Brendan's novel occurs when he is composing a scene in his head while walking down the street. He imagines his hero waiting in the hospital to hear of the birth of his child. Shortly after the reverie ends, he thinks of the fact that he himself is undergoing the birth process: "The man I am become in these past weeks is kin only to that old writer who, someday, sitting on a balcony in Nice or San Francisco, will try to think back to this year and this place, to the moment when he was truly born." (p. 130) The second reference to Brendan's book is a statement which the officer bringing news of Mrs. Tierney's death overhears Brendan making on the phone to his editor: "But in chapter fourteen, the paragraph about childbirth you don't like, I'm not sure about it, I think I'd like to leave it in." (p. 311) The announcement of the death of Brendan's mother thus coincides with the manifestation of Brendan's new identity as a writer (for he is making revisions on the accepted manuscript of a completed book) just as the death itself coincides with the completion of the book and its acceptance by the editor.

There are therefore three interlocked reasons for Mrs. Tierney's death in the novel. She dies because Brendan fails to make a phone call. She dies because of the justified wrath of God. She dies in the manifestation of the creative will of the novelist. In Moore's previous books the fantasizers have been passive and humiliated; in the crucial moment of their lives, each one is associated with the crucified Christ and the powerless child. In *An Answer From Limbo*, it is Mrs. Tierney as mother of children who is associated with Christ. When she falls at the beginning of her agony, the omniscient narrator tells us that "A crucifixion of pain shot down her leg from the thigh." (p. 270) Like Christ, she is tormented by thirst and headache, and like Christ she is absolutely abandoned. When she suffers her first stroke, the telephone hits her wrist "with the force of a hammer blow." (p. 286) The figure on the floor so dispassionately revealed to us by the omniscient narrator at the beginning of her suffering is both a grim parody of the figure on the cross and an embodiment of the sexual life of women, for her arms are raised as if she were making a gesture of love and submission, and her lower body is shamefully bared. The transfer of the suffering Christ pattern from the fantasizer to the mother of the fantasizer marks a change in Moore's view of himself as artist. No longer is the creating of fiction the act of the impotent and the weak; rather it is the mysterious act of the father. The fantasizer as novelist is both father and God.

In creating the book—a subsistent existing thing—the novelist creates himself and his own world. This action irrevocably alienates him from the actual world in which he lives, for from the moment of his birth in the new self-created identity as writer, the persons in the actual world cease to exist for him in their own autonomy. They become the subjects of his fantasy, figures to be observed and then used at need in the creation of books. The mysterious title of the book is explicable when we understand that the writer of the novel is as God. Those people from his real life whom he does not contemplate creatively in his fantasy are like the souls in limbo whom God does not contemplate. Thus at the book's beginning, Brendan summons from his mind the figure of his mother in response to his creative need, and at its end, he is the disinterested watcher of her funeral, storing up his memories of the event for future exploitation in his fiction.

The very proof of the novelist's power condemns him to a state of complete isolation or to a condition of inexpiable guilt. The impotent fantasizers who are Brendan's predecessors have one glimpse of their solitude in an empty and shapeless universe, and they return quickly to the rigidity and safety of the paternal system. Brendan faces that solitude more steadily than they do, yet he harbors the hope and fear that he is contemplated by the father as god. The narrator of "Preliminary Pages to a Work of Revenge" is addressing the father at the end of the story:

> Can you see me? Can you see the man who sits at a desk trying with a pen—that ludicrous weapon which conceit once forced into his hand—to reach you across the waste of twenty years? Look, look and you will see me. Here I am. I am here. Can you see me now? Do you laugh? Or do you weep?

Just before his book is completed, Brendan reflects that he is writing it for "some old Dog-God Father who will look down and tell me he is well pleased." (p. 247) The watching eye of the eternal father is the writer's only refuge from the horror of his own isolation. Indeed the proof of power and capacity to the father is the only justification for what the novelist has done in becoming a writer. And yet the assertion and proof of authorial omnipotence is a blasphemous challenge to God, just as it is an oedipal attack on the father. To prove himself as masculine creator, to make himself loved by the father as God, the novelist must perform the primary act of power, but in so doing he offends the very paternal power he is seeking to placate. If the man who remembers having been violated in the fountain does not so profoundly prove himself, the outrage of the violation remains unavenged, and he is consigned to the contemptible female role of the powerless. Thus the author of the story bleeds from the rectum at the time when he should have been recognized before the world as a great writer. If he does prove himself, he is like Brendan the lonely god of a solipsistic universe and the predator and scavenger on the lives of those whom he has an overwhelming obligation to love.

3

The Power of the Novelist

In his interview with Hallvard Dahlie, Moore remarks on a change in himself and in his circumstances which occurred between the writing of *An Answer From Limbo* and *The Emperor of Ice-Cream:* "I am much happier now than I was when I was thirty-five or forty. *Emperor* was written at a crucial time in my life—it was the first book after I changed." The change which Moore acknowledges in his life is clearly reflected in his fiction, not only in *The Emperor of Ice-Cream* (London, 1966), but also in the two novels which followed it. *The Emperor of Ice-Cream* shows significant changes in the recurring patterns of Moore's fiction. Once again he gives us the conflict between the fantasizer-son and the rigidly authoritarian father, but this time the conflict lacks the deep, driven pain characteristic of its earlier appearances, and the issue of the conflict at last is the reconciliation of father and son, the father's acceptance of the son's triumph. It is interesting that at this point in his career, the Christ-as-victim pattern disappears entirely from Moore's work.

The book's eighteen chapters, presented by a third-person omniscient narrator with special interest in

Gavin Burke, proceed chronologically through the months between November of 1939 and the bombing of Belfast in April of 1941. Moore counterpoints Hitler's conquest of Western Europe in these months with Gavin Burke's struggle against the emasculating paternalism of Belfast. The qualities Moore persistently associates with the father are divided between three men who dominate Gavin until the end of the book, when he at last defeats them and achieves his own manhood.

Mr. Burke, Gavin's father, is the center of order and stability in the Burke family. Stern and pious, he rules his children and his wife with absolute authority. The characteristic encounter of the elder Burke and Gavin involves the father standing at the top of a stairway like a condemning judge, (p.114), like God the father, (p. 189) while Gavin stands or lies at the foot of the stairs, disgraced by public failure or by drunkenness. The encounter ends with the father's expression of contempt for the son, while the son is filled with wounded love for the father, and impotent rage against him.

To Craig, the commander of the Air Raid Patrol post, where Gavin works, Moore assigns the sadistic component of paternal authority. Craig's name is the same as that of Sir James Craig, Prime Minister of Northern Ireland from 1921 to 1940, a man identified in Ulster politics with the repression of Catholics. As chief authority in the post, Craig revels in the arbitrary exercise of power. One of his underlings sadly remarks that Craig enjoys "shoving it into his fellow man as often and as hard as he can." (p. 126) Craig's lessons in first aid frequently involve the humiliation and sadistic punishment of the men. It is interesting that Craig is the only male at the post who is sexually involved with any of the women.

John Henry Moriarity, who appears in only one scene of the book, is a doctor. Moriarity seems to be the father as oedipal rival. He is gigantic in size, invincibly powerful, and Gavin's rival for the affections of Sally Shannon. At the Old Boys' Dance at St. Michan's, he takes Sally away from Gavin, and then humiliates the boy twice, first by causing him to show fear and then by an overtly sexual insult. John Henry's appearance is astonishing; he is over six feet tall with "a curiously unreal face, like a store dummy's, with shiny black hair lacquered to his skull, a pencil-thin mustache, rouge-red cheeks, and staring blue eyes, round and false as the weighted eyes of a china doll." (p. 161) By his name and his profession, he is linked to Moore's father, if not to Gavin Burke's.

The dividing of the father into these three figures is accompanied by a diminution of paternal power. John Henry's cartoon doll appearance and his lisp undercut the threat he offers to Gavin. The menace of Craig is vitiated by the speech mannerisms which Moore assigns to him and by the fact that Craig's authoritarian activity is a constant bizarre annoyance to those under his power, but never really a threat. Mr. Burke is discredited by the patent absurdity of his political views. The reader of a book which appeared twenty years after World War II was over cannot take seriously the self-righteous nationalist bluster of a man who keeps announcing that the war will last a few weeks.

Moore's treatment of Gavin Burke reveals a similar

diminution of pressure. Moore's deep ambivalence toward the previous fantasizer figures gives way in the creation of Gavin Burke to affectionate nostalgia. Gavin is a decent, good-hearted lad. He is consistently able to view himself with a kind of ironic detachment. The sophisticated moral intelligence which makes the ironic view of the self possible coexists in him with a more primitive child's morality in which he sees obedience and submission to the father and the church as good, self-assertion as evil. Moore assigns to Gavin a mental habit of envisioning himself in a struggle between the White Angel, who advises the goodness of the conventions, and the Black Angel, who advises satisfying the self. The Angels thus look suspiciously like superego and id, especially when they disappear to be replaced by "a new voice, a cold grown-up voice." (p. 250) Voila—the ego. The device of the angels, Gavin's habit of meditating on the mysterious ways of those whom he calls "grown-ups," his tendency to think that people are old if they are thirty remind us of the perverse immaturity of Judith Hearne. However Gavin is just within the acceptable limit of age which make such naiveté tolerable, and Moore clearly intends it as an attractive quality in his hero.

Gavin's problem is to release himself from the world dominated by the father. At the beginning of the book he expects this release to coincide with the destruction of the old order prophesied by the champions of the subversive world of the imagination—Yeats, Auden, and MacNeice—and about to be carried out by Hitler. Gavin wants Hitler to bomb Belfast because he wants to destroy his father and his father's world. The war for

Gavin is an event productive of "a shameful secret excitement, a vision of the grownups' world in ruins." (p. 7) He hopes for the destruction of Belfast because he thinks that only then will he be released from the rigid demands of authority and convention. Gavin is also convinced that the bombing of Belfast will allow him to prove himself sexually to Sally Shannon, the student nurse whom he loves. When his first attempt to seduce her fails, he stands on Cave Hill looking down on Belfast and wishing that the planes flying above his head were German bombers: "Here on the mountainside he would see it all, the explosions, the flames, the holocaust. From here, he would run down to rescue Sally, then on through the smoke and rubble to a hero's job in the First Aid Post." (p. 112) Sally Shannon, like Ginger Coffey's wife whose surname she shares, embodies the life Ireland will give to the hero.

In terms of the novel, the German bombs which flatten the city carry no heavier weight than Gavin's desire to become a man, that is to destroy the father and establish his own sexual maturity. When the bombs do at last fall, Gavin does prove himself by confronting death and, it would seem, his own oedipal fantasy. Gavin's testing in the stench and filth of the morgue lasts a whole day, but Moore gives us specific descriptions of only three of the bodies he touches. The first is that of a young woman, befouled by excrement, "the first naked body of an adult woman he had ever really looked at in his life." (p. 233) The second corpse is that of an old man. Gavin notes the ugliness of "the loose skin, . . . the veiny calves, the limp, somehow pathetic, genitals." (p. 233) The third corpse belongs to an R.A.F. officer, whose body Gavin sees is split down the middle from the neck to genitals. (p. 237) The three specified bodies form the oedipal triangle: the hidden body of the woman is revealed; Gavin sees its sexual mysteries which Moore once again associates with organic filth. The phallus of the old man—the father—seems weak and pitiful. Yet the body of the young man, wearing as Gavin does a British uniform, is mysteriously split "through some freak of air blast." (p. 237) Gavin in the house of death looks on the bodies of the mother, the father, and the destroyed son. Having done so, he enters the generational order as an adult male, and asks a kiss of Sally Shannon. When he sees that her prudery will never permit him to exercise his masculinity, he renounces her. Then he goes to his family's ruined house, and there forgives his father, who is pitiful and broken, but who confesses at last his love for his son.

The transformation of the omnipotent sadistic father into comic components and the frank authorial affection for the fantasizer hero are significant changes in this book which should be related, I think, to its weakness. The book is flawed by Moore's use of the techniques of narrative realism when he no longer has a view of the world which can be expressed by such a convention. The view behind the first group of Moore's fictions is that there exists outside the mind a world fixed and defined in eternal validity, created and ruled by paternal power. Against this rigid order, as we have repeatedly seen, the fantasizer builds an inner world, subversive of the true one, and therefore evil. The use of the Wallace Stevens poem to name this book suggests Moore's new perspective on the world, one in which the imagination is at last accepted as legitimate. The poem's view of mind, however, remains unarticulated in the form of the novel. The poem itself seems awkwardly used in the book. It is quoted in fragments (p. 8, p. 29, p. 232) at wide intervals in the book, but Gavin's understanding of it seems subservient to his delight in discovering that other people know the poem too. In the morgue scene, elements from the last stanza enter the narrative: Gavin sees an old woman's horny feet and the cold and dumb body of the young woman. The Irish nationalist Gallagher comes into the morgue to search for the bodies of his own family, having affixed the beam of his lamp into the night sky in an attempt to draw the bombers to the city, only after the event realizing that he will not be spared in the destruction he desired. One is tempted to draw a parallel between Gavin, the incipient artist as destroyer of family, and Gallagher, and the use of the poem in the book suggests that the parallel should be drawn. Yet Moore no longer seems to feel that the artist is a destroyer, and the parallel does not mean anything.

Moore's commitment to the moral system embodied in the patriarchal external world gives unusual power to the realism of his earlier books. A major function of the realism of those first four books is to conceal the figure of the novelist and to punish him for being a novelist. The legitimizing of the imagination of the fantasizer which has taken place between *An Answer From Limbo* and *The Emperor of Ice-Cream* drains the realistic convention of force. Brendan Tierney and Gavin Burke want exactly the same thing—recognition of their power as men. Brendan gets it by the death of Mrs. Tierney, which is presented in the book in scenes of horrifying authentic-

ity. Gavin gets it by the destruction of a city, yet the
scenes of disorder in the bombed city, indeed all of the
big scenes in the book, are emotionally empty. Moore is
clearly interested in writing a timeless fable of testing
and reconciliation which has particular significance for
himself as an artist. But Moore's fable gets tangled with
the trappings of a realistic novel: a very large cast of
characters, careful description of the physical terrain of
Belfast, and location in a specific and limited historical
period. In the earlier books, realistic elements are
charged with their own being and with hidden meaning
in relation to the fantasizer. In *The Emperor of Ice-Cream,*
they exist only as background for the testing of the hero
and they lose validity. If the earlier Moore had written
this book, we could not so easily accept that hundreds
should die in the service of Gavin Burke's liberation.

In *I Am Mary Dunne* (New York, 1968), the reader is at
every point made aware that the closely woven realistic
density of the novel is a triumph of the creative imagination. Moore's title echoes Flaubert's "*Madame Bovary, c'est
moi,*" and in so doing establishes the fact that the character Mary Dunne is the creation of the novelist Brian
Moore, and that in the character as artifact, he will
reveal himself. The epigraph of the book reinforces the
point: "O body swayed to music, O brightening glance,/
How can we know the dancer from the dance?" In this
book, the novelist will reveal himself in the practice of
his art.

The symmetrical shapeliness of the book draws further
attention to its artfulness. The first-person narrator,
Mary Dunne, at the end of a difficult day attempts to
recapture its "every single thought, word, and deed,"

(p. 4) and in the process recaptures her past. The book is Mary Dunne's act of memory, an act performed because she feels her identity about to disintegrate. She can locate herself as a person only in her ability to remember; thus she opens the book with a memory in which as a fifteen-year-old girl, she substituted in a class room discussion "*Memento ergo sum*," for Descartes' "*Cogito ergo sum*." The act of memory is also an act in which guilt is acknowledged. Indeed guilt is inseparable from remembering; thus the heroine initiates her Proustian feat with the formula of guilt from the confiteor of the mass, in which the penitent begs forgiveness for every evil thought, word, and deed.

The narrative is continuous, broken only at irregular intervals by wide spaces on the page. The first paragraph locks into the last, so that we discover at the conclusion that Mary has remembered while she lies in bed terrified and sleepless beside her third husband. Mary's thoughts move in chronological order through a series of encounters in the day just past; each encounter triggers in her mind either intricate fantasies of what might happen in the future or guilty memories of what has happened in the past, particularly in her first two marriages.

Her relationship with her first two husbands follows an identical pattern. Each one begins with a sexual encounter in a hotel room in which the man fails to perform adequately; each proceeds to an unsatisfactory marriage in which the man becomes increasingly weak, while Mary's ambition for a richer, more sophisticated life remains unsatisfied, as does her sexuality. Each marriage ends when a hostile female friend reveals to the husband that Mary is sexually involved with another man. Each marriage is officially dissolved when Mary goes alone to a distant city and endures the legal formalities of the divorce.

In her marriages Mary changes her name and her circumstances three times, and she does so through a more or less calculated use of her husbands. She did not love Jimmy Phelan, but married him to escape from Butchersville, Ontario. She married Hat Bell, doubting that she loved him, but also trading a drab life with a dull man for a glamorous one in Montreal and New York with a successful if alcoholic journalist. She marries Terence Lavery, genuinely loving him, but as his wife she enters a wealthy and sophisticated world. Through her marriages Mary has achieved success, yet she has done so by exploiting others and then betraying them. Thus her success, the satisfaction of her desires, can never be untangled from her guilt. In this respect, the marriages of Mary Dunne are the equivalent of Brendan Tierney's activity as a novelist. But Brendan and Mary live in radically different moral contexts. Brendan, whose subjective life feeds on the actual lives of those close to him, is alone in guilt. Mary however exists within a universe in which every person uses others in the service of inner fantasies. Through both the conscious thoughts of Mary Dunne and her experience, Moore presents a world in which every person is subject and object, exploiter and victim. People cast fantasies on Mary Dunne just as she casts fantasies on them. She uses men, and they use her. The constant changing of her surname in marriage is a metaphor for the double status of all human beings. In the role of object she accepts the identities which her husbands confer on her. Indeed she manipulates her appearance so that men will project fantasies upon her, yet she is bitter about "the silly degradation of playing pander and whore in the presentation of my face and figure in a man's world." (p. 31) As intelligent and sensitive subject, she recognizes herself as object to others.

A new attitude toward experience which Moore reveals in this novel permits him to view the creation of fiction, both in private fantasy and in the work of the artist, as a morally acceptable action. Since every person's perception and experience of the objective are seen to be shaped subjectively, the life in the mind is no longer a solitary aberration of the impotent and rebellious, but a universal fact of human experience. In *An Answer From Limbo*, Moore's sense of the fictional world as subversive of the real and the true caused him to present the novelist character as the destroyer of Mrs. Tierney. In *I Am Mary Dunne*, his more complex view of the interaction of the subjective and the objective in human experience permits him to present himself as novelist in the act of creating Mary Dunne.

There is evidence to suggest that Moore drew directly for that creation on the literature of psychoanalysis. He told Hallvard Dahlie while he was writing the book that he was influenced by Guiseppe Berto's *Incubus*: "That's the book I've enjoyed most in the last few years. It's written in a strange style—a sort of galloping monologue like a psychoanalysis where he tells all." Berto's book is about a neurotic author-narrator who suffers severe anxiety attacks after the death of his father, and whose suffering is alleviated by a successful psychoanalysis. Berto carefully and sympathetically explores the analysis, explaining the Freudian mechanism behind the hero's problems. In *I Am Mary Dunne,* Freud himself enters the book via one of Mary's fantasies when she sees an old couple in Central Park whom she identifies as Sigmund Freud and his wife. (p. 92–94) Mary feels her identity shattering into parts which, like Gavin Burke's angels, seem pretty clearly to be identified with the Freudian structure of the personality. These facts suggest that Moore's use of Freud's theoretical writing in the presentation of Mary is a definite possibility. In any event, Freud's paper on the anxiety neurosis and his case history of the hysteric Dora illuminate certain aspects of Mary's experience.

Mary reveals most of the symptoms Freud presents for the anxiety neurosis. Freud writes that general ir-ritability is a symptom and suggests sensitivity to noise as a manifestation of that irritability. Mary passes her day in a state of extreme nervousness which she attri-butes to premenstrual tension, and she is severely troubled early in the day by household noises. As a second symptom, Freud lists the anxious expectation of disaster to the self and to loved ones. On the day in the book, Mary expects her mother to die, expects to lose her own sanity, fears that her husband will commit her to an asylum. Freud writes that an actual anxiety attack is characterized by disturbances of heartbeat and breath-ing, by tremor and shuddering, by vertigo, and by sleep-lessness. Mary makes the act of memory because she is sleepless, and through the day she suffers repeatedly from every one of the disorders Freud mentions. Freud sug-gests that such attacks in married women are due to frustration at particular sexual inadequacies of their husbands. Mary's first two husbands between them had the three difficulties with potency which Freud considers. On the day of the book, however, Mary is in a happy marriage with a sexually competent man. Her distress is shown to have deeper sources than the frustrations of her past marriages. Repeatedly she returns to her discovery at the age of fifteen—the age she is in the schoolroom memory which begins the book—that her father died in a hotel room while in bed with a prostitute who abandoned him in death. She has created a detailed fantasy of the prostitute's acts in the moments preceding and following the death. She dreams of the scene, thinks of it, and repeatedly enacts it in her own sexual life. She feels like a prostitute when she prepares to give herself to a man, even to the loved husband Terence. She abandons the men as the prostitute abandoned her father. Her life with Hat Bell exactly repeats the central elements of the fantasy. She first gives herself to him in a hotel room and in the moment when she crosses the room toward him, sees herself as the woman who approached her father. She leaves Hat, having been warned that doing so might push him into suicide. The memory which is the book is formed on the day on which she learns that her departure from Montreal was followed by his suicide. Her suffering is not simply natural grief at the death of Hat, but overwhelming psychic pain which grows out of her feelings for her father. It is this deeper area of Mary's suffering that can be linked to Freud's case study of Dora. Dora's father was syphilitic; throughout Dora's adolescence he carried on an affair with a family friend. In his analysis of the girl, Freud showed that she felt that both she and her mother had been infected by the father's disease, which she felt to be both physical and moral. Like Dora, Mary blames her father for what she considers her evil sexual passions. Occasionally in her terrors, Mary transforms her loved mother into the disgusting companion of her father's pleasures; in that guise, she thinks of her mother as Big Gertie, a prostitute, and a song goes through her mind in which she presents herself as Big Gertie's prostitute daughter.

At the very center of the book, Mary presents a memory of terror which has certain remarkable similarities to the second dream in the Dora analysis. Mary remembers her first experience of the loss of identity, which occurred in a public square in El Paso after her Mexican divorce from Hat Bell. Her panic began when she reflected that for the moment, between marriages, she had no appropriate name; she saw three young Mexican girls staring at her, heard an evangelist shouting behind her back, and then completely lost the memory of her own name. She ran in panic till she came to the door of her hotel where she found her identity, seizing on the name her father gave her: "*I am Mary Dunne.*" (p. 109)

In Dora's dream as presented by Freud, the girl is wandering in a strange town, in one of the squares of which is a monument. She finds in the house in which she lives in the town a letter from her mother announcing her father's death. She returns home and hears from a maid that her mother and the family are at the cemetery. Like Dora in the dream, Mary is in a public square in a strange town. This square—as in Dora's dream—has a monument, to which Moore calls particular attention. The letter announcing the death of Dora's father may perhaps resonate in the lost letter from Ernie Truelove which announces the death of Hat Bell. Mary repeatedly thinks of the cemeteries in which her father and Hat lie buried; she collapses the two graves into one, particularly when she thinks of the phallic shape of the snow-covered grave stones. Freud analyzes Dora's use of the cemetery—by means of the German word for it—as a reference to defloration; the cemetery to Dora means intercourse. Mary does not have the linguistic associations to the word that Dora does, but the cemetery seems to mean intercourse to her also. At the end of the day, she thinks of the two cemeteries and prepares to commit suicide by leaping into a cleared building site—a white space enclosed by the wreckers in a wall made of old doors. The plunge into the space is the plunge into the grave of the dead father-husband; her death would be the symbolic act of intercourse.

Whether or not the influence of Freud on Moore's presentation of Mary Dunne is as direct as I have suggested, the fact remains that she is classically neurotic, as of course are Judith Hearne and Devine from the early Belfast books. These early neurotics, however, are viewed by Moore from an ethical standpoint. Through the fiction, as we have seen, Moore condemns them for doing what he as a novelist did—that is for living a life in the imagination and for failing to accept their places in the paternalist community. The use of narrative omniscience and the fidelity to the conventions of realism in the early books coincide with Moore's ethical view of the characters. In the later books, the identification of the fantasizer characters with Moore as novelist becomes clearer, but a major element impelling the fiction remains the moral condemnation of their lives. Moore's presentation of Mary Dunne shows that a humane tolerance has replaced the rigid moralism of the first four books. This new tolerance frees Moore to reveal in the book itself his own skill in the act of imaginative creation.

From the beginning of his career as a novelist, Moore has been a master of telling physical detail. In the first four books, this precisely rendered detail enforces the sense that the book is a mimetic image of an actually existing world. In *I Am Mary Dunne* because the narrative voice belongs to a woman, and we are conscious that the novelist is a man, we are forced to recognize the book's intricate realism as the novelist's creation out of observation and memory. The transformation of realistic detail from mimetic fact communicated by an impersonal omniscient narrator to imaginative creation of a novelist who uses the title of the book to enforce awareness of his role in it, is accompanied by the disappearance from the book of the Moore father type. "My father the lecher. My father who art in hell," (p. 64) thinks Mary of her father. The previous Moore fathers are puritanical, God-linked, order creating; the adulterous Dan Dunne is diabolical and by his absence the source of disorder and suffering in the life of his child. Mrs. Dunne cannot supply the protection against total solipsism and moral chaos which Brendan Tierney, in both fear and hope, receives from his father. Mrs. Dunne says to the distraught Mary, attempting to secure her daughter's identity in maternal love: "You're my daughter you'll always be the same to me." (p. 214)

But like Mrs. Tierney, Mrs. Dunne is caught in the brutal generational order—she lives in Butchersville and suffers from a rectal growth which may be cancerous. Not the flesh-bound mother, only the transcending father could save Mary from isolation. Thus after speaking to her mother, Mary attempts to find her father in the suicide gesture. But the grave-bed where she looks for him is empty—a waste ground defined only by the absence of what was once there, its walls of doors leading to nothing. Alone in disintegrating terror at the end of the book, she summons the memory of her day and her life, and in that solitary subjective act claims from chaos her identity, which is, no matter what, created by and linked to the absent father: "I am Mary Dunne." (p. 217)

The central issue of Moore's work from this sixth novel onward is the absence of the father; that absence and the consequent subjectivity of all experience are associated by Moore with the popular media. Television and film become important elements in his work, either as influences which resonate in it, or as matters directly considered in the narrative. I would suggest here that one more element seems to operate in *I Am Mary Dunne*— the John Huston film *Freud*, which was released in late 1962. In that film, one of Freud's female patients has a powerful fantasy of discovering the dead body of her father in a house of prostitution. None of Freud's case studies contains such material. It seems reasonable to suggest that Huston's film may have had some influence on Moore when he invented the circumstances of the death of Dan Dunne.

The media element is submerged in *I Am Mary Dunne*,

but it is very clearly operative in Moore's next book, *Fergus*. (New York, 1970) The novel explores the objective and subjective experience of a single day in the life of Fergus Fadden. Fadden is Gavin Burke grown up and Brendan Tierney grown older. He is a Belfast writer of thirty-nine with two novels and a broken marriage behind him, living in California while working on a film script. On the day which the book presents, Fadden has a series of hallucinations in which he sees with baffling sensual completeness all the persons whom he has ever known and who have thus passed into his memory.

Fadden's life in California follows the patterns of mass entertainment: of television situation comedy and of the films Hollywood used to make about itself. He lives with a beautiful twenty-two-year-old girl named Dani Sinclair, whose motives, feelings and ideas are totally mysterious to him. On the day which the book presents, Dani's mother Dusty, a failed actress and a working beautician comes to visit. At dinner Mrs. Sinclair tells Fergus of the role she as an actress would like to play: "a Lucille Ball situation. Attractive older woman, maybe in a comedy segment." (p. 115) Mrs. Sinclair's visit is just such a comedy segment: pseudo mother-in-law confronts embarrassed lover of her daughter on a day on which the lover is troubled with second sight. In his sit-com domestic life, Fadden plays the victimized bumbler, who is also a nice guy. In his B movie working life, he plays the artist as victim of heartless tycoons. He is writing for two literally fabulous movie magnates. Redshields, his director, is the master of all sensual pleasures; he is simultaneously vulgar and

decadent, ruthless in his ambition and his desire to ex-
ploit everyone exploitable. Boweri, his producer, is huge
and androgynous, enormously wealthy, the claimant to
the blood of all nations. Moore names the pair for
maximum effect. Each one is associated with failure:
New York's Bowery and the Salvation Army's second-
hand stores. The assignment of such names to such men
seems calculated to reveal their falseness. At the same
time, the names capture a truth: their emptiness, the
real poverty at the core of their wealth.

Boweri and Redshields, Dusty and Dani are non-
persons. Fergus cannot make human contact with any
of them. By means of the four, Moore suggests that
California is a waste land. Indeed Fergus remembers
the lines about Mrs. Porter and her daughter from *The
Waste Land* once when he thinks about Dusty and Dani
(p. 107), though he does not remember that the preceding lines present Sweeney on his visit to Mrs. Porter in
the spring. Dusty and Dani summon another Eliot pair
and another Eliot work in which Sweeney appears—
Dusty and Doris of *Sweeney Agonistes*. Eliot's unfinished
play, with its epigraphs about seeing avenging ghosts
and searching for God underlies Moore's book as
surely as does the idiom of mass entertainment. In
Eliot's play, the murderous, guilty, memory-ridden
Sweeney erupts into the vacuum occupied by Dusty and
Doris and their vulgar companion-clients. Fergus is
Sweeney in the California vacuum. The Fergus who
cries, who is dependent on Dani and intimidated by
Redshields and Boweri—Fergus the media hero—
coexists with the Fergus who is associated with the
hero of Eliot's strange play.

The key to the significance of the *Sweeney Agonistes* association in Moore's book is to be found in Fadden's memory of a solitary night visit as a schoolboy to the ruins of Doe Castle in County Donegal. The Castle, which incidentally is two miles from Creeslough, the site of Mrs. Tierney's girlhood home, was the fortress of the MacSweeney family. In the sixteenth century, the fortress was the scene of a number of battles between the MacSweeneys and their rivals. The boy Fergus in the courtyard of the Castle "had looked up at the ruined keep from which men had been flung to their deaths in the bloody days of MacSweeney NadTuath." He was overcome by terror, "sure that he was being watched, sure that the ghost of MacSweeney would strike him dead for having ventured into his domain . . . " (p. 121) The boy in terror at having usurped the place of a powerful masculine spirit, who is watching and who will destroy him—this is the configuration of guilt and fear which, as we have seen, drives Brendan Tierney and destroys Devine. And indeed Moore brings *An Answer From Limbo* and *The Feast of Lupercal* into this novel. Like his predecessors, Fergus made his peace with the powerful ghost by withdrawing from Ireland into the imagination. His own name expresses a retreat, for Fergus is the deposed king in the sagas of the Ulster cycle whom Yeats presented in a poem admired by Stephen Dedalus as a man who left the real world for the world of dream. What Fergus realizes on the day of his revelations is that he is the source of his own guilt and fear, that the tragically tormented Sweeney element of his being, is like his life and his work, his own creation.

If the outer life of Fergus is conducted among shades

in the waste land, his inner life has the complexity of true human involvement. The hallucinated persons who move through his day have the substance and weight of the real. They are fully and minutely observed by the omniscient narrator, but the reader is repeatedly reminded in the text that the apparitions are created in the mind of Fergus on the basis of his memories. Confronting as a sixteen-year-old girl in California, his sister Maeve, who is actually forty-two and living in Ireland, Fergus announces that she is his creature. "I'm the one who imagines you there, eating that plum right now. At the moment, you're my invention." (p. 54) The apparitional Maeve raises the question about the artist's illusion of omnipotence, which in one way or another has concerned Moore throughout his career, and leaves behind her a real pit from the plum. Fergus meditates on the sensual completeness of his visions and then thinks he can wilfully, "like some necromancer," conjure them up. The omniscient narrator articulates directly in good psychological terms what is going on: "He did not even put his thought into words; it translated itself from a pre-speech area in his brain into an instant materialization of Mrs. Findlater. . . . " (p. 78)

The apparitions in the early part of the day establish the facts of Fadden's Belfast past and in so doing link him to the heroes of the other Belfast books. The early apparitions, as we have seen, are recognized by Fergus as the embodiments of his own fantasy; he forgets that his own mind is the creator of presences so overwhelmingly real as the apparitions become more menacing in the course of the day. From evening into night, Fergus stands accused in a series of progressively more frightening judgment scenes. In the first, his younger self, arrogant in inexperience, conducts a trial, the main issue of which is the relation of the literary ambitions of Fadden's youth to the achievements of his middle age. The trial shows that the pretensions, deceits, treacheries of Fadden's life can only be justified by the value of his work, but the judgment of his work is withheld; the accusers disappear.

Later in the evening, Fergus finds himself going to confession to a priest from his old parish church in Belfast. Here the issue is the opposition between the Catholicism of his early life and his desire, as an agnostic, to do literary work of unquestionable objective value. The accusing Father Byrne is immediately replaced by Father Keogh of St. Michan's. Between *The Feast of Lupercal* and *Fergus,* Father Keogh's punitive authority has ceased to be spiritual; he beats Fergus as the boys at St. Michan's were beaten by his rebellious underling, Father McSwiney. (In the light of the Sweeney association, it is worth remembering the younger priest's name and his position as antithetical double of Dev in *The Feast of Lupercal.*) In the hallucinated encounter, Fergus seizes the cane and beats the old man till the priest cries out for mercy and Fergus realizes his own sadism: "I am just like they were, . . . I am no different. I stood there yelling with pleasure as I beat him. I could have killed him." (p. 127)

Before the final and terrifying trial, Moore places a skillfully managed encounter between Fergus, Dusty, and Paddy Donlon, a friend of Fergus who is dead, possibly by suicide. Fergus moves in conversation between the living woman, who can hear only Fergus, and the

dead man, who can hear Fergus and Dusty. Fergus and
Paddy Donlon discuss the difference between a view
which interprets reality in subjective terms and one
which interprets it objectively. Against the self-righteous
moralism of Donlon who insists that "A man is what he
does, not what he says he does," (p. 163) Fergus argues
that what matters in our judgment about other people is
what we think they are and do.

In the great scene on the sand dunes which closes the
book, we have Moore's recognition of the terrible loneliness which accompanies that accepted subjectivity.
This scene surely echoes the work of Fellini, the cine-
matic master of scenes of reconciliation and terror at
the edge of the sea. Here Fergus descends into the limbo
of the remembering and imagining mind, where the
thronging masses of people remembered wait for him,
many of them with hatred. The occasion is the family
picnic on the beach with which the Fadden family
customarily celebrated the birthday of Fergus. At the
picnic the shadowy throng works itself from accusation
to ritualized attack. The mob focuses its hostility on
Fadden's inability to remember a particular woman, a
woman who is actually beaten by the crowd and whose
skirt is stripped off. Fergus momentarily saves himself
from mass fury by asking for his father, but he knows
that he can protect himself and the woman only if he can
remember who she is. When the mob attacks again, this
time stoning the girl, the family refuses to help him, and
Fergus to save the girl must flee with her. On their flight,
he at last remembers her, and we learn that she is a woman of no particular importance in his life. Years
before, he had introduced her to the man she later mar-

ried; Fergus had been best man at her wedding and godfather to her child. The only thing of which Fergus is guilty in relation to Elaine Rosen is forgetting her.

The savage treatment accorded to Fergus and the girl by the crowd is the psychic creation of Fergus himself. Simply as a woman, Elaine Rosen draws from him a sadistic response; this response in turn makes him guilty, the worthy victim of his own avenging punishment. The beach associated in Moore's imagination with the birth of the hero in this book, with the betrayal of the father in *An Answer From Limbo,* with abandonment by the father in *The Feast of Lupercal,* is the fitting site for the embodiment of this central fantasy. Yet primitive sadism has nothing to do with Fadden's actual relation to Elaine Rosen, a relation of civility and friendship in which he clearly respected her independent reality as a person, no matter what image he projected on her in the hidden depths of his consciousness.

The book ends with the acceptance of isolation in subjectivity and of the unapproachable independent complexity of those persons who play the chief parts in Fergus's private inner drama; most particularly, Fergus sees his father as simply a man. Pushed to the extreme edge of his existence by the heart attack which follows his encounter with Elaine Rosen, Fergus approaches his father and hears the words which justify his own life as an artist when his father tells him that we must live and die on earth in the boundaries of our own experience, (p. 226) that we create the significance of our own lives: "If you have not found a meaning, then your life is meaningless." (p. 227) Having tasted his own death, Fergus can at last demythologize his father, accept him as a man, release him from the role of tyrant and god he has held for so long in the depths of his son's being.

4

The Novelist as Revolutionary and Conservative

The two works which have followed *Fergus* show that this reconciliation with the father, this renunciation of the ordered world are not for Moore definitive. In his next two books the struggle between the father and the child remains central, but the stronger force now becomes the rebellious younger generation. The fathers—three politicians in *The Revolution Script* and an aging abbot in *Catholics*—are beseiged and defeated by revolutionary youths in the media-dominated universe, which signifies to Moore isolation in subjectivity and the depletion of moral value.

The fictionalized documentary, *The Revolution Script* (New York, 1971) is the most flawed and disturbing of all Moore's books. Its explicit concern with media is nothing less than obsessive. The book appeared hard upon the actions which it chronicles: the 1970 kidnappings of James Cross and Pierre Laporte by FLQ terrorists in Montreal. In an introductory note, Moore writes of the kidnappings as media super-events. He presents the objects of his particular concern, the kidnappers of Cross, as leading actors in that media pageant. "Even in the last act of this drama," he writes of their televised flight from Montreal, "they still seemed shadows, figments of our imagination, fleeing into exile and silence." Moore presents his book as an attempt "to bring these young revolutionaries on the stage" by means of the techniques of fiction. We have here an extraordinary enterprise: to rescue the revolutionaries from their media-conferred fantasy status, they will be presented in a literary fantasy—a fictionalized narrative, the main actions of which Moore perceives as a drama. Objective reality has collapsed.

Moore shows repeatedly that his revolutionaries see themselves as heroes in a media drama. Their inspiration and model for action is *The Battle of Algiers*; they are fascinated with their personal power over television and radio programming and with their role in a great televised spectacle. What is more disturbing than the naiveté of the revolutionary characters as Moore presents them, is the simplicity of his mode of conceptualizing the action they perform. He sees them as noble children in revolt against the repressive political and social forces which have twisted and tragically limited their lives. The narrative emphasizes the youth of the kidnappers, either by direct statement or by implication from the kinds of actions and statements it ascribes to them. The urge to project youth, enthusiasm, and innocence on them corrupts the book in conception and in language. The kidnappers of Cross are presented gently joking in their hideout, tirelessly instructing each other on the media as an instrument of guerilla terror, engaging in the chaste pleasures of married love or the most sentimental of love affairs. We are shown the group watching the announcement on television of a government concession to their demands: " *Nous vaincrons!* " Jacques said and, around the television set, they all raised clenched fists. They had begun to hope." (p. 53) At another triumph, one of the revolutionaries exults: " 'Okay, you goddamn ruling authorities, there's the voice of your people. Let's open up the jails. Algeria here we come!' "(p. 144)

In opposition to Moore's noble youths in this dramatic script are three middle-aged men: Cross and Laporte, who are their victims, and Pierre Trudeau, who is their vicious enemy and rival in a battle conducted for and on the media. Moore's quite clear identification with the kidnappers is matched by a less obvious one with this trio of aging men. Moore was in fact, like Cross and Laporte, forty-nine years old in 1970; Trudeau was forty-eight. Cross, Laporte, and Trudeau are shown to have more than their age in common: all were successful; all were betrayers of nationalist causes—Cross because he was Irish-born and yet a servant of the British government, Laporte and Trudeau because they were French Canadian and powerful in a government under which French Canadians were systematically deprived and degraded.

Montreal—the place where Moore's first successful novel was written—seems to be the symbolic locus for him of a struggle between success, which involves selling out, and failure, which involves fidelity to a limited and deprived national background. Moore's trio of successful men constitute the Gerry Grosvenor element of *The Revolution Script*; their success is punished by the outraged child-revolutionaries, just as Grosvenor, the image of Ginger Coffey as a successful man, is punished in the earlier Montreal book. But the choice of Montreal as the site for this act of retribution has another significance. The urban terrorist activity which must have been of overwhelming interest to Moore in 1970 was being carried out in Belfast. For Moore, Montreal is fantasyland; the real war is in Belfast. In an article "Bloody Ulster: An Irishman's Lament," which appeared in *The Atlantic Monthly* (September, 1970), Moore welcomed the arrival of British troops in Northern Ireland, because he felt they were the only force which could prevent the slaughter of the Catholic population. Moore's radical politics are for a make-believe world; in relation to the overwhelming reality of Belfast, he must advocate order-preserving conservatism.

Seen in the light of Moore's previous work, *The Revolution Script* is clearly an exercise in projection: Moore's historically existent revolutionary youths and middle-aged men, disembodied by the media, distanced from him by nationality, are given in the book a shape of particular significance to Moore. There is something unethical in this projection of the deeply personal onto public events involving real persons. The subject matter of Moore's book demands the scrupulous impersonality of the journalist, not the private emotional energies of the novelist. This naive and self-indulgent book sentimentalizes and degrades Moore's constant and honest preoccupations. We are given precisely what the title promises: the script for a media melodrama in which there are heroes and villains, and in which human suffering is reduced to a cheap cliché. "The hearse moved off on Pierre Laporte's last automobile ride, the journey to the grave." (p. 182) Such casual brutality is only possible in a context from which all of the weight of common humanity has disappeared.

In *Catholics* (New York, 1973) Moore restores the hierarchically ordered objective world which he attacked in the first phase of his career and disintegrated in the second. In this most recent of his books, he approaches a structured and divinely sanctioned world from the viewpoint of the order-giving father, rather than that of the rebellious child. It is true that he presents that world at the moment of its disappearance, but the fiction is ordered to show that the disappearance is the ultimate proof of that world's validity. *Catholics* is quite literally an apocalyptic book, and apocalypse as Moore conceives it depends on the existence of God and of the Roman Catholic Church. The book is set in the 1990s; the ominous year 2,000 hovers just beyond its range. The Roman Catholic Church, committed to ecumenism and social change, is about to absorb yet one more world religion—Buddhism. (As every Catholic school child used to know, just before the last day, there will be one fold and one shepherd.) Images and lines from Yeats's "The Second Coming" flash through the book, and a helicopter out of Bergman's apocalyptic *Through a Glass Darkly* violates Muck Island with its inhuman menace.

Once again, Moore brings together a conservative Ireland and an authoritarian Rome, but this time the previous meanings of the configuration are altered. Rome has renounced the old mysteries and rituals, to involve itself in the world of daily actuality. Muck Island, off the west coast of Ireland, clings to the Latin Mass, to all the old ways. Rome in the interests of uniformity and obedience sends James Kinsella, a young priest who does not believe in God and who sees the church as an instrument of social change, to bring into line Tomás O'Malley, the sixty-nine-year-old Abbot of the monastery on the island. Rome intrudes because television, that associate of destroyed moral value for Moore, has interested itself in the Irish religious ceremonies.

The omniscient narrator divides his attention between the cold and subtle Father Kinsella and the Abbot. Both are decent men, but it is the suffering and humane Abbot who is the hero of the book. The struggle between Kinsella and the Abbot is hardly a struggle; the Abbot capitulates quickly: "Because it is my duty to obey." (p. 95). That statement reveals his acceptance of an order which is hierarchical and paternal, and which overrides the desires and even the best judgment of the individual person. To Kinsella, the Abbot is a son; to the monks in his monastery, however, he is a father; he demands of the monks the same obedience he gives Kinsella. "Insubordination," he reflects: "The beginning of breakdown." (p. 86) The Abbot will neither offer nor tolerate insubordination. He sees the monastery as a community of children under his command. And indeed the life on the island has the order and beauty of the life of a child in a loving household. The goodness of the food on the island is an index of the goodness of the life there. The Abbot is a stern father who sends the monks to work and to bed on careful schedule, but he loves the monks and at the end of the book, he enters into his own torment in order to protect them.

The Abbot leads the monks in the recitation of the

Our Father before the tabernacle in the abbey church; in so doing, he resigns himself to a state of blank despair, "a sort of purgatory presaging the true hell to come, the hell of no feeling, that null, that void." (p. 81) We have seen this state before, not only in Mary Dunne's terrors, but also in the glimpses of the self lost in chaos which most of his other fantasizer characters have seen. There are new dimensions, however, to the Abbot's experience of this horror. First, he undertakes it out of love, rather than suffering it as some sort of punishment. Secondly, the whole apocalyptic structure of the book suggests that the Abbot's fear of God's nonexistence is unfounded, for the world is preparing for its destruction just as orthodox Catholicism taught that it would. In effect this book studies the breakdown of the world structure identified with the religious teaching of Moore's youth in such a way as to assert the enduring validity and vitality of the structure. Thus the Abbot's heroic suffering is not his final condition; by implication, it will be justified in its ending.

In this book, Moore returns to the old view of the world as objective and ruled by God through a human network of fathers, and to Ireland for setting. The media paradigms for experience, as used in *Fergus* and *The Revolution Script*, have vanished, their only trace the Bergman helicopter. This book is intensely literary; in it Moore seems at pains to join himself to the great Irish writers who opened the century which his book implies is the last one. Moore's Abbot is a hawklike man, (p. 38) a man like the old artificer whom Stephen Dedalus recognized as his father. Yeats's "Second Coming" is closely woven into the language of the book, and Synge's journal of life on the Aran Islands is woven into both its content and its language. Moore at fifty-two seems at peace, for the moment, with all fathers. Like the Abbot, he seems to be now in the world of the father, which is a complex and mysterious new one, waiting to be explored.

Selected Bibliography

WORKS CITED IN THIS TEXT

Judith Hearne. London: Andre Deutsch, 1955.
The Feast of Lupercal. Boston: Little, Brown and Company, 1957.
The Luck of Ginger Coffey. Boston: Little, Brown and Company, 1960.
An Answer From Limbo. Boston: Little, Brown and Company, 1962.
The Emperor of Ice-Cream. London: Andre Deutsch, 1966.
I Am Mary Dunne. New York: Viking Press, 1968.
Fergus. New York: Holt, Rinehart and Winston, Inc., 1970.
The Revolution Script. New York: Holt, Rinehart and Winston, Inc., 1971.
Catholics. New York: Holt, Rinehart and Winston, Inc., 1972.

CRITICAL STUDIES

Cronin, John "Ulster's Alarming Novels," *Éire-Ireland IV* (Winter, 1969): 27–34.
Dahlie, Hallvard, *Brian Moore*. Toronto: The Copp Clark Publishing Company, 1969. (This study contains biographical information and bibliography on Moore's work and criticism of it through *I Am Mary Dunne*.)

Foster, John W. "Passage Through Limbo: Brian Moore's North American Novels," *Critique* XIII (Winter, 1971): 5–18.

Prosky, Murray. "The Crisis of Identity in the Novels of Brian Moore," *Éire-Ireland* VI (Fall, 1971): 106–118.

Studing, Richard. "A Brian Moore Bibliography," forthcoming in *Éire-Ireland*. (This is a complete bibliography of Moore's work, including the pulp fiction, and of the criticism of Moore through December 1974.)